BLEEPS AND BLIPS TO ROCKET SHIPS

Great Inventions in Communications

ALANNAH HEGEDUS & KAITLIN RAINEY

ILLUSTRATIONS BY BILL SLAVIN

TUNDRA BOOKS

For Tim

A.H.

For Jillian

K.R.

For my father, who fixed radios and televisions for a living but would rarely fix ours – so I had to draw

B.S.

Published in Canada by Tundra Books, *McClelland & Stewart Young Readers,*
481 University Avenue, Toronto, Ontario M5G 2E9

Published in the United States by Tundra Books of Northern New York,
P.O. Box 1030, Plattsburgh, New York 12901

Library of Congress Control Number: 00-135461

Canadian Cataloguing in Publication Data

Hegedus, Alannah
Bleeps and blips to rocket ships : great inventions in communications

Includes index.
ISBN 0-88776-452-5

1. Inventions – Canada – History – Juvenile literature. 2. Communication – Canada – History – Juvenile literature.
3. Telecommunication – Canada – History – Juvenile literature. 4. Inventors – Canada – Juvenile literature.
I. Rainey, Kaitlin. II. Slavin, Bill. III. Title.

T23.A1H43 2001 j609.71 C00-932281-7

We acknowledge the support of the Canada Council for the Arts and the Ontario Arts Council for our publishing program.

We acknowledge the financial support of the Government of Canada through the Book Publishing Industry Development Program for our publishing activities.

Printed and bound in Canada

1 2 3 4 5 6 06 05 04 03 02 01

Contents

Chapter 1

Fenerty and the Invention of Newsprint

From ancient times, people have recorded their thoughts and ideas by engraving them in stone, tracing them in wet clay or on wax-covered wooden tablets, or writing them with ink on parchment, **vellum**, or **papyrus**. Leaves from trees and bark were also used as a writing surface.

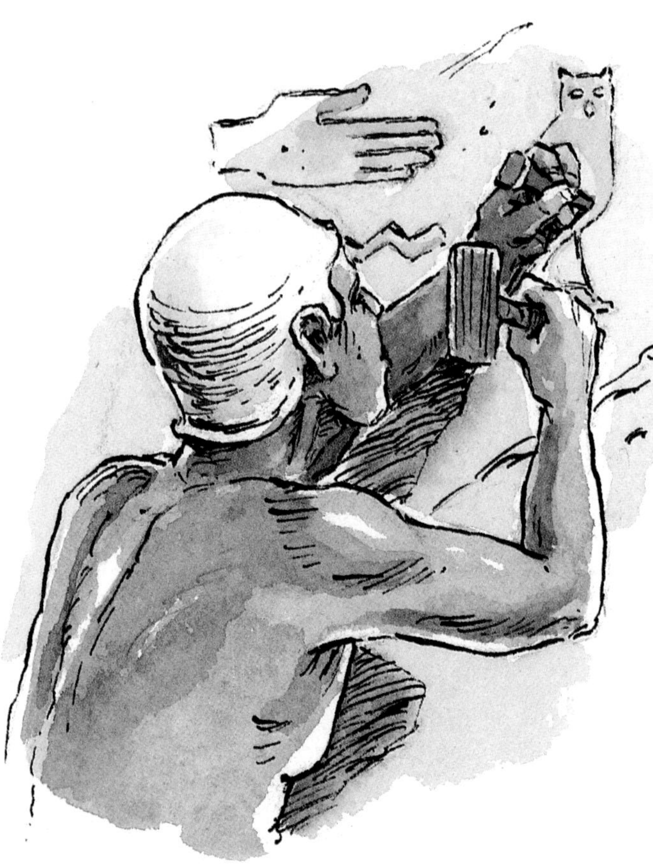

Today we use paper. For centuries, paper was made by hand from cotton or linen from old clothing, bedding, or other household goods. These rags were collected and chopped into a mash before being formed into sheets on a rectangular mold, pressed, and hung to dry. Paper made from linen was particularly high quality because of its strong fibers, which came from the flax plant. In fact, flax straw is so strong that on the North American prairies, where it is commonly grown, farmers burn piles of flax chaff rather than till it under the soil because it breaks down too slowly.

When the papermaking process was first mechanized, in 1817, it became possible to

Did you know that in 1666, the British Parliament ordered people to begin using wool funeral shrouds so that cotton and linen could be saved for papermaking?

How Paper Was Made Before Automation

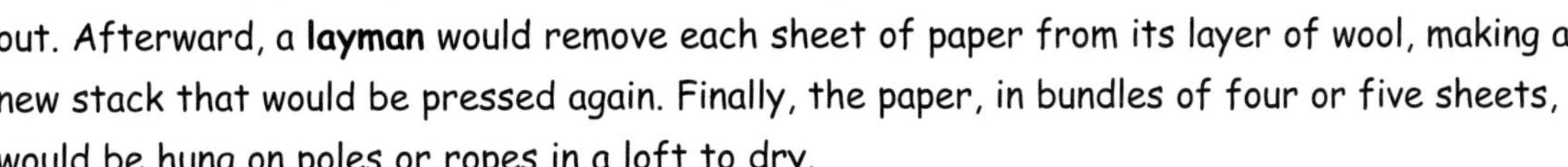

Once the cotton or linen rags had been cleaned and beaten to a pulp in a stamping machine, water and the broken-down cloth fibers were combined in a vat. The **vatman** would dip a mold into the resulting mash and lift out a layer of wet fiber. (In Europe, the mold was made of closely spaced wires; the more traditional Asian-style mold was a basket-like mesh of bamboo or dried grass laced together with horsehair.) The vatman would then hand the mold to the **coucher**, whose job it was to drain off the extra water and remove the sheet of paper by turning the mold upside down over a piece of wool felt. He would stack more than a hundred sheets, with a piece of felt between each one. This pile of damp paper would then be put in a press to have the water squeezed out. Afterward, a **layman** would remove each sheet of paper from its layer of wool, making a new stack that would be pressed again. Finally, the paper, in bundles of four or five sheets, would be hung on poles or ropes in a loft to dry.

produce large quantities of paper quickly. The demand grew, and soon the supply of rags could not satisfy the papermakers' requirements. A new kind of raw material was needed.

Charles Fenerty of Halifax, Nova Scotia, had an idea for a good, cheap source of papermaking fiber. He was only a teenager when he proposed that wood could be ground up finely and reduced to the same kind of pulp used in the nearby Holland Paper Mill, where he had seen the process of papermaking and heard about the shortage of rags.

When he was growing up, Fenerty worked in his father's sawmills. He observed that some of the sawdust produced by the huge saw blades in the mill became mashed into a filmy gauze by the movement of the powerful equipment. In 1838, he began experimenting with ground-up wood to see if it was possible to make paper from it. Imitating the workers at the paper mill, he broke down the fibers using water and friction. For a mold, he used a basket with a closely woven bottom, a tool not so different from that used for centuries in China. He then pressed the paper with an iron spoon to remove moisture and compress the fibers.

Fenerty's method differed from traditional papermaking in that he used only wood pulp

Did you know that the shortage of rags became so serious that newspapers urged women to sew decorative work bags to hang in their parlors so that every scrap of old fabric could be saved for monthly collection by the ragman? One merchant advertised that "1 1/2 pounds of rags will buy a primer or a story book, or one yard of ribbon, two thimbles, two rings, twelve good needles, two strings of beads, one penknife, etc."

Make Your Own Paper

Recycle some old paper to make new sheets that are either white or colored - you can even add glitter or other extras to make creative patterns. Gather all the equipment first, and make sure you have a clear space near the sink to work.

You will need:

- a blender
- an electric iron
- a stapler
- a plastic washtub
- several pieces of felt (about 10 x 13 inches [25 x 33 cm])
- an old towel
- a sponge or a cotton rag
- a wooden orange crate (or build a wood frame that measures 8 x 10 inches [20 x 25 cm])
- 3 pieces of plastic window screen (about 14 x 18 inches [35 x 45 cm] each)
- sheets of paper to recycle

Getting Ready

The first thing you will need to do is to make the mold. If you have an old orange crate, ask an adult to help you remove the bottom and then stretch one piece of window screen across it and up the sides. Staple this securely in place, taking care to bend the staples smooth if they stick out. (If you don't have an orange crate, ask an adult to help you build a frame with thin pieces of wood.)

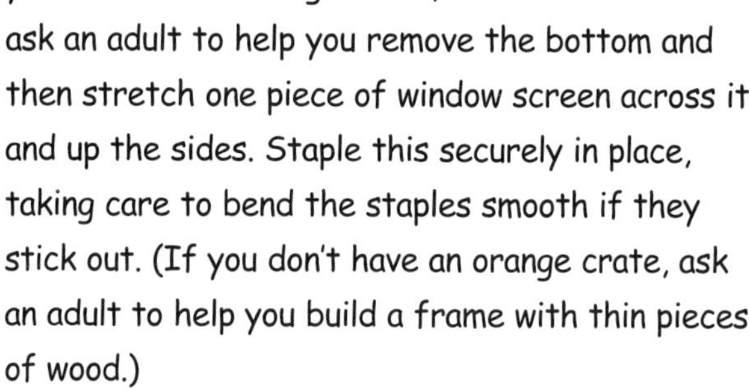

The second piece of window screen will be the removable layer on which the paper is made. Trim this screen to be a bit larger than the bottom of the crate and press it neatly inside. Cut the third piece of screen to the same size and save it for later.

and did not have the equipment necessary to apply constant pressure to flatten the sheet he had formed. It took many attempts to produce a good-quality result. Sometime between 1838 and 1840, however, he succeeded in producing paper that was of the same quality as that made from cotton or linen rags. He recommended that papermakers use fir, spruce, or poplar, because these woods were more fibrous than others.

Making the Paper

Set up your workspace by placing a towel next to the plastic washtub and the mold inside the tub. Measure out the following ingredients:

- 1 1/2 sheets of paper (8 1/2 x 11 inches [22 x 28 cm])
- 1 small square of colored paper (3 x 3 inches [8 x 8 cm])
- 3 1/2 cups (875 mL) of water

1. Rip the paper into pieces and place them in the blender with the water.
2. Put the lid on and run the blender at high speed until the ingredients turn into pulp (roughly 30 seconds).
3. Pour the pulp into the mold, letting the excess water drain into the tub.
4. Jiggle the mold a bit to spread the pulp evenly on the screen. (This is when you can sprinkle some glitter or other bits of decoration onto the wet pulp.)
5. Lift the mold to let all the water drain off into the tub. Place the dripping mold onto the towel.
6. Set a piece of felt on the counter. Lift the paper out of the mold by picking up the corners of the screen. (The paper is still too fragile to handle by itself.) Lay the screen on the felt and put the third piece of screen on top of the paper (so that it is sandwiched between two pieces of mesh).
7. Use a sponge or dry cloth to press as much water out of the paper as possible. Dry it as well as you can so the paper will be strong.
8. Gently remove the paper from the screen and lay it between two pieces of felt. Press it flat.
9. If you like, you can now make more sheets of paper, until you have several pieces layered between squares of felt, drying out.
10. The final step is to iron your paper smooth with a hot, dry iron (no steam). Ask an adult to help you with this job. Lay the paper on the ironing board and cover it with a piece of cotton fabric (like a tea towel). Iron carefully until the paper is dry.

Fenerty did not think of patenting his papermaking process, and it wasn't until 1844 that he published a letter in his local newspaper about his findings. He felt that wood pulp could easily be turned into quality paper, and he hoped that scientists would do further experiments to verify his findings. Unfortunately, his letter didn't stimulate much interest in Canada.

Meanwhile, German inventors had responded to the shortage of rags in their country by developing and patenting both the process and the equipment required for making newsprint from wood pulp. By 1852, more than ten years after Fenerty first had his idea, wood pulp was being turned into paper in the Voelter Mill in Heidenheim. Commercial production of ground-wood paper in North America was still another twelve years off.

Did you know that in 1719, René Réaumur of France proposed that people should be able to make paper from wood just like wasps do? During the 1700s, others suggested using materials such as seaweed and swamp moss.

Fenerty is the first person in North America to have made paper from ground wood, but he was not the first in the world. In the 1760s, Dr. Jacob Schäffer of Germany experimented systematically with everything from wasp's nests and corn husks to pine cones and cabbage stalks – and of course, wood. A few decades later, in England in 1800, Matthias Koops patented a method of making paper from a number of substances, including wood and bark. He demonstrated his results by putting together a book with some pages made from straw and others made from wood alone. Koops was the first to manufacture paper commercially using fibers other than cotton or linen. His mill, where paper was made by hand, primarily used straw as the raw material.

Though change eventually came, Fenerty's experiments with wood pulp did not attract the attention he had hoped for among local papermakers. After spending some time in Australia and New Zealand, he settled in Halifax, where he did some farming, worked as a lumberman, and served the community. He had a lifelong interest in nature, and together with his wife spent his leisure time studying plant life and gardening, but he never returned to papermaking.

Chapter 2

The Photograph Gets Published: Desbarats and Leggo Invent the Halftone

On October 30, 1869, people visiting newsstands in Montreal saw something totally new. Stacked among the countless type-laden newspapers and magazines was the first issue of the *Canadian Illustrated News* – with a photograph of Prince Arthur, Queen Victoria's son, splashed across the front page. For more than forty years, people had been trying to publish photographs, but Georges Desbarats and William Leggo were the first to succeed. Their invention, the **halftone** reproduction of a photograph, changed printing and publishing forever.

Seeing the World in Shades of Gray

Before the halftone, any pictures in newspapers, magazines, or books were hand-drawn interpretations of events. Often the picture was inaccurate, and the process of making and printing these illustrations took a long time. Illustrations regularly appeared long after the event they depicted had occurred.

There were three different types of printable illustrations: **lithographs**, which artists made by drawing on stone slabs with greasy ink; **woodcuts**, produced by hand-carving a picture into a wooden block; and **engravings**, made by using chemicals to dissolve the areas around an image's lines. Because each of these processes was time-consuming and expensive, publishers all over the world wanted to find a faster and easier way to reproduce images.

In the 1820s, a French physicist named Joseph Nicéphore Niepce invented the photograph. This discovery heightened the race to find a fast, efficient way to accurately mass-produce illustrations. People experimenting in this area, in fact, were so competitive that they worked in secrecy, afraid to share their discoveries and ideas with others. But despite all the competition, and some small successes reproducing black-and-white images and line drawings, no one was able to reproduce a photograph, with all its shades of gray.

Finally, in the 1850s in England and France, the first halftone screens were developed. Early screens were pieces of transparent paper ruled with tiny squares all over the sheet. By rephotographing a photograph through the screen, engravers could break it down into thousands of tiny pieces, each one corresponding to one of the squares on the halftone screen. Among those who were interested in developing this new technology further were Georges Desbarats, a visionary with an idea for photographically illustrated journalism, and William Leggo, an engraver.

A Family Business

Unlike many inventors, Georges-Édouard Desbarats came from a wealthy family, so he had the advantage of being able to finance and pursue his ideas himself. He was born in 1838 in Quebec City to a family that had run successful printing businesses for more than two hundred years. But Desbarats did not intend to carry on the family business. Instead, he studied to become a lawyer. After completing his law degree, he traveled to Europe and visited Pau, France, the town where his family had originally lived. In a small shop, he found and bought a book that had been printed in 1686 by one of his ancestors. Visiting Pau and finding this book must have greatly affected him, because when he returned home, he decided to work part time with his father, learning all about the printing business. Eventually, Desbarats gave up law altogether and worked full time in printing.

In early 1864, the government of the United Provinces of Canada (this was pre-Confederation) moved to Ottawa. Desbarats's father, Georges-Pascal Desbarats, moved with it, building a printing plant in the new city. Now he had printing operations in Quebec City, Montreal, and Ottawa, and when he died later that year, Georges-Édouard moved to Ottawa and took over the business.

Desbarats's father was a practical businessman, but Georges-Édouard was an "ideas man." He was fascinated with inventions and new technology. He had seen photographs, and knew they were a powerful communication tool. He wanted to be able to publish them. And as a printer, he wanted to find a faster, less expensive way of mass-producing illustrations on paper. In the early 1860s, in Quebec City, he met William Augustus Leggo, an engraver who shared his interests.

Because of all the secrecy that surrounded printing and engraving in those times, we do not know much about Leggo. What we do know is that his family was from Europe, he was born in 1830, and his father was an engraver who learned lithography from its inventor in Germany and taught his trade to his four sons. By 1860, Leggo and his brothers were living in Quebec City and working in a family business called Leggo & Co.

Like Desbarats, Leggo was fascinated by new ideas. The two men decided to work together. They made a good team: Desbarats provided the financial backing, and Leggo had the technical knowledge about engraving and photography. By 1865, they held a joint **patent** for **Leggotype**, a photoengraving process that allowed them to reproduce line drawings. This invention was the first stage in finding a way to reproduce photographs, and Desbarats and Leggo were confident they would succeed. Then tragedy struck.

From Tragedy to Triumph

One of Desbarats's good friends in Ottawa was Thomas D'Arcy McGee, a politician who spoke out against the **Fenians**, a secret Irish-American organization devoted to Irish independence. On April 6, 1868, McGee was assassinated by a Fenian on the steps of his boardinghouse, which Desbarats owned. Desbarats placed a plaque in his friend's memory on the house, even though he received anonymous threats warning him not to. Then, on the night of January 20, 1869, arsonists set fire to his printing factory. The blaze destroyed everything. It is believed that Fenians set it to drive Desbarats out of business because of his support of McGee.

But Desbarats would not give up. Luckily, he had left a copy of the printing plates for the complete works of the explorer Samuel de Champlain, twenty volumes of writings, illustrations, and maps, with his editor in Quebec City. This gave Desbarats, who was determined to rebuild his business, something to print immediately. In fact, he used Leggotype to print the charts and maps.

Still, Desbarats knew he could never replace all the printing plates he had lost in the fire, so he began to think about new business ventures. Quickly, three things came together in his mind. First, he realized that the maps and illustrations he had used with Champlain's writings helped communicate the man's adventures more clearly and in less space than words. Second, he realized that photographs are even more realistic than drawings, and therefore would have even more impact. He believed that readers would enjoy seeing realistic depictions of events and people alongside news stories. He also thought that photographs would sell more magazines. And finally, he realized that Canada had no national magazine. Desbarats was proud of Canada, and he wanted to publish a magazine featuring Canadian art, nature, people, and events. This would not only appeal to Canadians, but also demonstrate how much was being accomplished in the new country.

Desbarats shared his vision with Leggo. Since they were already working on a way to reproduce and print photographs, they increased their efforts, worked even more hours, and devoted themselves to this goal. By July 1869, Leggo was successfully printing halftone reproductions of photographs and working on improving the process. The men knew that they were almost ready to make history.

On October 30 of that year, Desbarats launched the *Canadian Illustrated News,* the first publication in the world with photographs in it. Desbarats and Leggo had at last realized their dream of publishing a halftone photographic reproduction.

Just as Desbarats had planned, the *Canadian Illustrated News* celebrated Canada. It contained news, sports and business reports, literature, gossip, fashion, advice, recipes, and a children's column. As well as Canadian news, it covered foreign news and literature, especially from Europe. Canada was a young country, and most people still had close relatives living overseas, so readers wanted to be informed about world events.

For fourteen years, from October 30, 1869, to December 28, 1883, the *Canadian Illustrated News* was published. During those years, it

Did you know that Desbarats foresaw "facsimiles" of newspapers? He believed that one day, people would be able to send copies of foreign newspapers, perhaps via telegraph, to North America, where they would be bought by residents who were from these countries originally or had family still living there. Current electronic technology allows whole pages and sections of foreign newspapers and magazines to be sent over long distances and printed in that location – or even read onscreen!

Desbarats's Other Publications

Desbarats published many magazines. Shortly after launching the Canadian Illustrated News, he started L'Opinion publique, a sixteen-page illustrated French magazine. The two publications shared illustrations and articles when they were of interest to both groups of readers, but L'Opinion publique was very much a separate magazine. It had its own editors, the foreign news was mainly from France, and the literary materials were by French and Québécois writers. This was another accomplishment for Desbarats, because "bicultural" publishing (publishing in two different cultures) was uncommon then, and still is today.

Desbarats also published many trade magazines, including the Canadian Patent Office Record, Mechanics Magazine, and the Canada Medical and Surgical Journal, as well as scholarly editions of rare books, biographies, music, poetry, criticism, essays, humor, and government documents.

covered the key events in the history of early Canada, including Louis Riel's Red River Rebellion, the creation of the Province of Manitoba in 1870, the construction of the transcontinental railroad, and Prince Edward Island's joining Canada in 1880. Today, the *Canadian Illustrated News* is important for historical researchers because it contains photographs and illustrations that are sometimes not available anywhere else.

Reflections of Canada

In the first issue of the Canadian Illustrated News, the editorial described Desbarats's vision for his new magazine. It read: "A Canadian illustrated paper would be as it were a mirror that would reflect Canadian nature, enterprise and art throughout the world. . . . By picturing to our own people the broad dominion they possess, its resources and progress, its monuments and industry, its great men and great events, such a paper would teach them to know and love it better, and by it they would learn to feel still prouder of the proud Canadian name."

About Halftone Photographic Reproduction

Why was Desbarats and Leggo's invention so important? They found a way to use light to transfer a photograph onto a printing plate and mass-produce it on paper. Their method works by dividing a picture into many tiny black dots. When we look at the reproduced picture, our eyes merge the dots so that we see only one whole image with many different shades of gray. You can see these dots by looking at a newspaper photograph through a good magnifying glass.

To make the halftone, Leggo used a halftone screen he developed, two photographic negatives (one with an image and one clear), a chemical solution, and light. To make the screen, he etched a grid of tiny squares onto a piece of glass. Each square worked like a pinhole camera: it took a picture of the tiny area in front of it, and shot according to the tone (the amount of light or shadow) of that area. So when Leggo placed the negative with the image in front of the screen and sent light through to the clear negative, each square created a dot of varying darkness or lightness. The original photograph, in other words, got divided into thousands of black or clear dots of different sizes. Areas with lots of big dots looked dark, those with smaller dots looked lighter, and those with very few dots appeared very light or almost white.

Next, Leggo rinsed off the new negative, which he had earlier coated with the chemical solution. Where the light passed through, the solution had solidified, but the rest of it just washed off. This left a firm, raised image, like a rubber stamp. Leggo attached this to a printing plate, inked it, and printed it onto paper. This is how he discovered that black ink and white paper could produce a copy of a photograph and show all the shades of gray. Desbarats and Leggo quickly patented this photoengraving process as an improved version of Leggotype.

Desbarats and Leggo Take On the World

The success of the *Canadian Illustrated News* inspired Desbarats and Leggo to find another way of benefiting from their invention before other printers started copying it. When, in

Create Your Own Halftone Image

You can use patterns of dots in four colors of paint to create a full-color picture, just like printers do with dots of ink.

You will need:

- a strong magnifying glass
- pictures from a newspaper, a magazine, or a comic book
- at least 8 cotton swabs, with the cotton removed from one end of 4 of the swabs
- yellow, red, blue, and black paint (tempera paint works best, but you can use any other kind too)
- white paper
- newspaper or plastic to protect your work area

To Create Your Picture

Cover the top of a table or other flat surface with the newspaper or plastic. Place your white paper on the surface in front of you and set up your paints. Take off the lids and pour some of each paint into each one. Use two cotton swabs (one with the cotton removed from one end) for each color. This will give you two sizes of dots to use.

Cut out some pictures to copy from the newspaper or magazine. Set them up with the magnifying glass somewhere that's not too close to the paint. Look at the printed picture through the magnifying glass so you can see the dots that create it.

To copy the picture, decide what color and area you want to start with, and then dip a cotton swab in that color of paint. Dab the swab onto your paper to make many dots. Follow the shape of the area in the printed picture you are copying. To get bigger dots (and thus more color), use the end of the swab with cotton on it. Put the dots very close together, but do not overlap them. For very tiny dots (and thus less color), use the end of the swab without cotton on it.

Repeat this process with each of the four colors. Remember that these four colors can be combined to create other colors (yellow and red make orange, for example, and blue and red make purple). Experiment with combinations to create all the colors you'll need. When you're finished, you'll have a full-color picture formed entirely from patterns of dots.

A Newspaper for Escaped Slaves

Mary Ann Shadd was born a free black woman in Wilmington, Delaware, in 1823. The Shadds wanted their children to be educated, but Delaware was still a slave state, and black people did not have access to schools there. So the Shadds moved to Pennsylvania when Mary Ann was ten. After attending a private Quaker school, she became a schoolteacher and taught other black people. (Most black people at the time had no education.) But in 1850, the United States Congress passed the Fugitive Slave Law, which held that free black people could be returned to slavery. Like many others, Shadd moved to Canada for her own safety.

At the time, there was only one Canadian newspaper devoted to black refugees. The Voice of the Fugitive was run by an escaped slave named Henry Bibb, but the paper promoted segregation (keeping black people and white people apart). Shadd believed strongly in equality, integration, education, and self-sufficiency. She understood the plight of the American slaves because her family had operated a "station" of the Underground Railroad, and had helped many black people on their way north to freedom. Shadd believed that black people in Canada needed an alternative to Henry Bibb's newspaper, and she was determined to provide that alternative.

Shadd knew that she would need to hide her identity to publish her new paper, because women were not supposed to give opinions or hold positions of authority. She convinced Rev. Samuel Ward, a respected and well-known black activist, to lend his name to her paper, but she did all the work. In 1853, she founded the Provincial Freeman, which she also edited and wrote for. Mary Ann Shadd was the first black newspaperwoman in North America.

Published weekly, the Provincial Freeman was an anti-slavery, anti-racist newspaper designed for Canadian blacks and refugee slaves. It carried articles on integration, equality, immigration to Canada, and women's rights, and it represented a positive view of black activities, culture, and success in Canada. Since escapees often became separated from each other on their journey north, Shadd also included pleas for information on relatives' whereabouts to help reunite families. The paper ran from 1853 to 1861.

November 1871, the *American Newspaper Reporter* printed an article describing their accomplishments in printing photographs and combining them with text, they knew they needed to act quickly. Their new version of Leggotype was fast enough to include photographs of news events with daily reporting, which had never been done, but producing it was expensive. They decided to launch a new newspaper in a large city where many people would buy it, and they wanted to act while they still had the new technology to themselves. They chose New York City, but they needed money to finance such a large endeavor.

Desbarats and Leggo formed the Union Art Publishing Co. in May 1872, and on May 4, they placed an ad in the *Canadian Illustrated News* inviting people to invest in "New York's first illustrated daily newspaper." The ad claimed that the newspaper's illustrations "would be produced from day to day, while public excitement, enthusiasm, or indignation were still at their height."

Many people were skeptical. They did not believe that anyone could attend an event one day and include an illustrated report of it in the paper the next. There just was not enough time. But Desbarats and Leggo persisted, and on March 4, 1873, the *New York Daily Graphic* hit the streets. It was the first illustrated daily newspaper in the world. For five cents, readers got an eight-page newspaper containing current news, entertainment, and gossip, with line drawings and photographs. Within the first year, the *New York Daily Graphic* had a daily circulation of thirty thousand. It ran from March 4, 1873, to September 23, 1889.

By the 1890s, publications all over the world were using the halftone. Now we cannot imagine a newspaper without photographs. Desbarats and Leggo were only able to reproduce photographs of local events, of course, and only in black and white. Today, however, we can take color photographs, send them all over the world, and reproduce them quickly. Still, if you look closely at today's printed photographs, you will see dots and know that it all began with Desbarats and Leggo's halftone.

Did you know that Desbarats sponsored a balloon crossing of the Atlantic Ocean? It was an 1873 publicity stunt for the New York Daily Graphic. Unfortunately, the attempt was unsuccessful, and Desbarats lost money.

Did you know that both the Canadian Illustrated News and the New York Daily Graphic failed financially but still gave Desbarats his greatest satisfaction? Even though they never became wealthy or famous, Desbarats and Leggo changed printing and publishing forever, and contributed greatly to history.

J.R.C
ULT
THE DAILY GRAPHIC
THE DAILY GRAPHIC
THE DAILY GRAPHIC
THE DAILY GRAPHIC

Chapter 3

Taking Pictures in a Circle: Connon and the Panoramic Camera

Five-year-old John Connon used to watch his photographer father, Thomas Connon, work in the darkroom. When John turned twelve, his father gave him a corner of the darkroom and developing supplies to use in his own photography. From then on, father and son worked side by side.

Thomas was constantly experimenting with ways to improve cameras and photographs. At the time, photography was a complicated art. Photographers had to prepare a light-sensitive emulsion (which is a mixture of liquid chemicals), coat a glass plate with it, place the plate in plate holders, put it all inside a camera, and take a picture by exposing the plate to light before the emulsion dried. Then the photographer had to develop the picture before too much exposure to oxygen ruined the chemicals.

Every picture used its own glass or metal plate, which meant a photographer had to carry a lot of big, heavy equipment. It was easier for people to come to a photography studio to have their picture taken. Photographers also had to be very skilled at knowing how long to expose the plate (that is, to let the light in through the lens). Today's cameras are automatic, but early cameras needed a long time to take a picture. Sometimes it took many seconds, even minutes.

One day, John entered the darkroom and saw pages of notes and diagrams beside his father. Thomas told John that he thought it would be an improvement if photographers didn't need a plate for each photograph. Instead, they could spread the light-sensitive

Did you know that some early photographers put people's necks in clamps to keep them still for the time it took to expose the plate? If the subject moved, it would ruin the picture, and the photographer would have to start all over again.

gelatin emulsion on a strip of flexible material, then roll it past the lens, like a roll of ribbon, for each picture. At the other side of the lens, it would roll around a holder. After each picture, the photographer could wind the film along to the next unexposed piece. Instead of needing a new plate for every picture, photographers could take many shots before they had to change the film. The photographer could then remove the entire roll, stretch out the exposed film, and develop the negatives.

Thomas sketched his idea on paper to show his son a full roll of film at one end and an empty roll at the other. He also calculated that cameras could be made smaller. John pointed out that the camera needed two other rollers, one at each front corner, so that the film would always stay the same distance from the lens. His father sketched these new rollers in. Only one thing was missing: a way for the photographer to know when to stop winding the film along after each picture. All at once, Thomas remembered a machine that wound yarn at the local woolen mill. He told his son, "After so many turns, it rings a bell or goes snap." His rollers needed something like that so photographers would know when they'd wound the film far enough.

Excitedly, Thomas wrote to the Toronto firm from which he bought photography equipment. He described his invention and included a detailed drawing of it. Unfortunately, the company replied that the film holder would just be too expensive to sell in Canada.
Four years later, in 1885, *Scientific American*

The Famous Historian

John Connon was not only an inventor and a photographer, but also a historian and a journalist. In fact, he is most famous for his book The Early History of Elora and Vicinity. People used to travel for miles to meet and speak with Connon about history and his inventions.

Connon's love of history came from his mother. His grandparents were two of the first settlers in the Elora area, and his mother was the first white child born between the Grand River and Lake Huron. During the 1880s, his father's health declined, so in 1883, when he was twenty-one, Connon opened a grocery store to help support the family. Other shopkeepers didn't appreciate people standing around and talking in their stores, but Connon was fascinated by the stories the older people told about local history. His store became a local hangout, and people began bringing him old documents and historical items. Connon continued to collect them his whole life, and many of them eventually wound up in his book.

Make Your Own Pinhole Camera

Before the invention of photography, scientists and artists used a camera obscura (Latin for "dark chamber") to record images made by light. The first camera obscuras were dark rooms with a little hole in one wall. Light came in through the hole and projected a huge image onto the opposite wall, where it could be traced by an artist. Because light travels in straight lines, the rays were inverted. In other words, the reflected image was upside down and backwards. Cameras still work on this principle.

Records show camera obscuras being used as long ago as the seventh century. Eventually, people developed small portable camera obscuras. These were dark boxes with a pinhole at one end and a sheet of ground glass at the other. Artists would put thin paper over the glass and trace the reflected image. Later, a mirror was placed in the box and the ground-glass plate was put on top (in place of the lid). The light rays reflected off the mirror, flipping the image right side up. This made it much easier for people to trace the image.

You can make your own camera obscura. You will need:

- a large, empty, clean tin can without any sharp edges
- a small nail
- a hammer
- wax paper or tracing paper
- tape
- black construction paper
- an elastic band

To Make Your Camera

Use the hammer and nail to pierce a hole in the center of the closed end of the can. Place the wax paper or tracing paper over the mouth of the can. Make sure the paper is smooth and tight, with no creases or folds. Wrap it tightly against the sides of the can, taking care not to tear the paper, then put the elastic band

magazine described a new American invention: a film roll-holder. It was the same as Thomas Connon's. He wrote to the Toronto firm, asking for his original letter back. Someone at the company remembered receiving it, but a search couldn't find it anywhere. John Connon discovered that the American inventor didn't have any scientific knowledge of photography. It seems likely that an employee from the Toronto firm stole the letter – and Thomas Connon's idea with it! Eastman Kodak used the new holder in its cameras and revolutionized photography, but Thomas Connon never made a penny.

Like Father, Like Son

Like his father, John Connon was interested in inventing photography equipment. But he had learned from Thomas's experience, and he around it to hold it in place and tape the ends to the can. This will be your viewing screen.

Next, wrap the black construction paper as tightly as you can around the end of the can where the paper is, so it forms a tube that extends at least 10 inches (25 cm) past the viewing screen. Tape the construction paper tube to the can. This acts as a shield to keep outside light from falling on your viewing screen and interfering with the image.

Now you're ready to use your camera obscura. Point the hole in the can toward a bright scene and look into the black tube at your viewing screen. If the scene is bright enough, you'll see an upside-down, backwards image on your screen.

The hole in the can acts as a lens. Light reflects off the scene, enters your camera through the lens, and hits the paper at the other end. This produces the image you see.

To trace the image, remove the black construction paper tube. Secure the can to a flat surface with modeling clay or by taping two pencils along the outside of the can, parallel to each other and about 2 inches (5 cm) apart. Cover your head and the viewing screen with dark material and, if necessary, hold the can with one hand while you carefully use a pencil to trace the image with the other. You'll probably want to be sitting comfortably in a chair, because this may take a while.

WARNING: Do not use your pinhole camera to look directly at the sun.

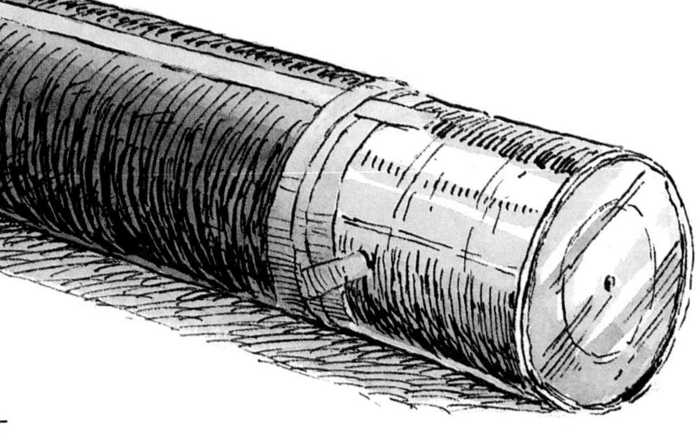

never demonstrated his inventions until he had filed patents for them.

His first invention was a new kind of **shutter**. At the time, cameras had shutters either in front of or behind the lenses, and these types of cameras were used only for quick exposure when there was a lot of light. But Connon's shutter fitted between the two lenses, and it could be used for both quick and long exposures. A tube with a rubber bulb attached operated the shutter. When you pressed the bulb, air pushed open the shutter so light passed through without being blocked. When you let go of the bulb, the shutter closed and a spring catch held it tight.

Did you know that John Connon was an amateur astronomer? He spent many hours in his garden looking at the stars through his powerful telescope, and even found a way to take pictures through it.

Developing Film in a Box: Arthur McCurdy and the Portable Developing Tank

In 1886, Arthur McCurdy, a newspaperman in Baddeck, Nova Scotia, became Alexander Graham Bell's private secretary and assistant. Bell decided that one of McCurdy's duties would be to photograph his experiments, since he wanted to have pictures as visual proof of his work. Bell sent McCurdy for lessons, and soon he was photographing all of Bell's experiments.

Bell gladly shared his enthusiasm for inventing with his friend. McCurdy was always interested in mechanics and figuring out how things work. One day, he was developing film at a local photographer's. He watched as the photographer placed the film on a pair of rollers and rolled it in the developing fluid. Seeing the rollers triggered an idea for McCurdy: he'd build a small portable tank that would fit around film rollers and act as a tiny darkroom. Photographers could take it anywhere with them and develop their own photographs quickly, and it would appeal to the steadily increasing number of amateur photographers.

Excitedly, McCurdy told Bell and his wife about his idea. Mabel Bell was so enthusiastic that she invested her own money in McCurdy's experiments. Before long, he had a working prototype and was ready to apply for a patent. Unfortunately, the examiner insisted that the principle behind McCurdy's portable tank was the same as that of a darkroom, so it couldn't be called a new invention. He was going to take some convincing.

While McCurdy worked on getting his patent in Washington, D.C., Bell was back in Baddeck. He wanted McCurdy to come back to work with him. If not for Mabel Bell, McCurdy would have done as Bell wanted. But Mabel believed strongly in McCurdy's invention, and she wanted him to have the time he needed to get his patent accepted. She continually wrote to her husband, stressing the importance of the portable developing tank and the need for McCurdy to stay in Washington to convince the examiner of the invention's value. She even arranged for another man to travel to Baddeck and work for Bell until McCurdy could return. Mabel Bell was certain the portable developing tank was a good idea, and she often told her husband that Arthur McCurdy ought to make a fortune from it.

Finally, in 1890, McCurdy was granted a patent. He called his portable developing tank Ebedec, which is the Native name for Baddeck. To thank Mabel Bell for her support and belief in his invention, he presented her with the first working model of his tank. That tank is on exhibit to this day at the Alexander Graham Bell Museum in Nova Scotia.

Did you know that Connon and his father liked to hike around their local area taking nature photographs? John also took outdoor photographs with groups of people in them, and these soon became a kind of trademark and a popular tourist attraction.

Connon made a camera with this kind of shutter and took a picture of a bridge being taken apart and the logs falling into the river. He opened and closed the shutter so quickly that he got a clear image of the action of the logs falling. Even though Connon didn't attempt to patent this shutter until 1890, eight years after he had first invented it, it was still a new idea, and he got his patent.

One summer day in 1886, Connon stood outside in his hometown of Elora, Ontario, preparing to take a picture of the scenery. He wished he could take a photograph that would show the view he saw as he turned around in a circle. Early panoramic photographs were difficult to produce and not very effective. A photographer would have to move his camera after each picture to get a sequence of photographs all the way around. When the photographer developed the photographs, he would join each one in the series to the edge of the previous one to create one long picture showing the whole view.

On that summer day, Connon simply took a picture with a regular camera. But how beautiful it would be, he thought, if he could capture the whole village. He started doing experiments, and he'd discuss his results and any problems with his mother and father and ask them for their ideas.

Perfecting the Panoramic Camera

To test his idea for a panoramic camera, Connon took a big empty box that had held tins of Keen's Mustard. Inside, he put a piece of bromide paper in the shape of a semi-circle. The lens was in front of the midpoint of the semi-circle. Between the lens and the paper he put a narrow box. It was attached to the camera box by hinges, and it swung like a very small hollow door to create a narrow aperture for light to pass through to the paper. To take a picture, Connon moved the lens from one side of the camera to the other. His experiments worked!

Seeing Double

As the panoramic camera turned, it took a picture of the photographer unless he ducked down below the lens. And it took so long for the camera to go around a circle that sometimes kids would play a prank. They'd be in place at the front of the line of people when the camera started, then they'd quickly run to the end of the line as it turned. This way, they'd end up in the picture twice! Unfortunately, people in the middle often turned their heads to watch the others run past, so the sides and backs of their heads got in the picture instead of their faces.

Did you know that panoramic photographs from Connon's camera were two and a half feet (75 cm) long?

When he was examining his results, Connon discovered a way to get a camera to rotate in a circle and take a picture all the way around. After light passes through a camera lens, it crosses over, then continues to the film, where it makes an upside-down image of the original scene. The point where the light crosses is called the **focal point**. Connon found that if the point around which a camera revolves is also the focal point, it will take a picture without blurring – no matter how fast the camera moves.

Using this principle, Connon designed a panoramic camera that would take a full-circle photograph. Inside, he loaded unexposed film onto a roller in front of the **focal plane**, a new technique. The film passed through a combination of four rollers, which held it securely along the focal plane. As the film was exposed, it wound onto a roller on the other side of the camera. Connon invented automatic controls that matched the movement of the film to the camera's movement, and he mounted the whole thing to a type of wheel that had a groove all around it. Connon would turn a crank to move the camera one way, and a cord loop would automatically move the film rollers the other way at the right speed. The whole apparatus sat on a tripod to support it and keep it steady.

The First Full-Circle Photographs

Once Connon finished designing the camera, he enlisted two local craftsmen to build it. By

February 1887, his camera was ready and it was time for him to try out his invention. The only place in Elora where he could get a full view of town in every direction was the top of a building owned by his friend Col. Charles Clarke. When Connon asked if he could take a photograph from the top of the building, Clarke said he was coming to watch. The two men climbed up to the roof, where Connon set up his new equipment. Then he took the first true panoramic photograph. The first picture worked, but Connon, who had to guess at the speed to turn the camera, was too slow and had overexposed the image.

He went back to the drawing board to find a way to fix the turning speed of the camera. He quickly developed a different system that used a clock-spring mechanism, then he and Clarke went to the rooftop to try again. This time Connon got a better result. The second picture was great.

Clarke had joked that Connon shouldn't take a picture from the roof of his building until he could take one of the whole view all the way around, and he insisted on being with Connon when he took his pictures. He was so excited about it, in fact, that he even went with Connon to develop the pictures afterward. It's a good thing, too, because in 1895, a person in Philadelphia challenged Connon's claim to the panoramic camera. When Connon wrote to Colonel Clarke, his friend said this about the first panoramic photograph: "I saw it taken. It still exists. It can be readily reproduced and is a durable proof of the excellence of your revolving camera." It turned out to be important that Connon had a witness to his invention the first time he used it.

A Move to New York

Connon received patents from the United States in August 1887, Britain in May 1888, and Canada in November 1888. He then set off for New York City, seeking financial backing to manufacture and sell the camera. He made sample pictures and showed them around. One company was interested, but it kept delaying a decision. It turned out that large photographic houses were threatened by this new technology and didn't want it to become easily available.

Finally, another photographic supplyhouse agreed to back Connon. He changed the crank to a draw cord, and in February 1890 the company sold his camera as the Wonder Camera. Just when the camera was released, new transparent celluloid film came on the market. Until then, Connon had been making his own film by coating light-sensitive paper with beeswax. He received one of the first shipments of this new film, and it was just what he'd been waiting for. He used it in the Wonder Camera, and the camera worked perfectly. Sadly, the film was too wide for the cameras that were already made, and before the company could fix the problem, it went bankrupt.

Connon kept working in photography, but in 1891 he decided he'd spent as much time and money on his panoramic camera as he could. Years later, he wrote that "the panoramic camera was just too soon for its time."

John Connon and his father never earned much for their inventions. But Connon did eventually get some recognition, and today we know him as the sole inventor of the panoramic camera.

Did you know that Rev. Hannibal Goodwin of Newark, New Jersey, invented transparent celluloid film? He filed for a patent on May 2, 1887, but a corporation convinced officials to keep delaying the patent while it marketed the film for its own profit. The United States Supreme Court eventually ruled that Reverend Goodwin was the inventor, but he died in poverty in 1900.

Did you know that when John Connon returned home from New York City, he worked for an electrical company to support his family? There he invented a dynamo (a generator) to drive a lighting system in a mill. One of his dynamos was used every night for twenty years in a local flour mill.

Did you know that John Connon began to gain recognition for his photography inventions only in the 1970s - more than forty years after his death!

Chapter 4

The Transatlantic Telegraph Cable Joins the Old World and the New

If you needed to send a message long distance in the 1830s, your letter would probably have taken a ride on a stagecoach and likely on a boat or a ship. In more remote areas, it might have been carried by a runner or transported down a river by canoe. Of course, there was no telephone or radio in those days, so people depended on these different modes of transportation for their news. By 1835 Samuel Morse had developed a working model of an electric telegraph, and in 1838 he devised the system of dots and dashes that became known as Morse code. The telegraph made it possible to send a coded message across a length of wire.

It wasn't until 1844 that Morse got support from the U.S. Congress to build the first telegraph line, but a new era was beginning, and rapid communication across great distances quickly became a reality. In the period that followed, the telegraph and the railroad grew up together in a network of lines that linked major cities across North America and throughout Europe. It was during the early days of this new technology that a Canadian inventor, Frederick Newton Gisborne, first imagined extending a cable across the Atlantic to link Europe to the New World.

In 1847, Gisborne, a descendant of the famous scientist Sir Isaac Newton, decided to learn more about this promising invention. He had completed his studies in electricity, engineering, and the sciences some years earlier, and after traveling the world, he decided to leave his home in England for Canada, where

Did you know that a Nova Scotian named Fred Creed found it so tedious to punch Morse code onto paper tape that he invented a typewriter-like machine to do the job automatically?

Did you know that Samuel Morse started out not as an inventor but as a portrait painter?

How Did the Telegraph Work?

Messages to be sent over telegraph lines were translated into Morse code in the form of holes punched into a tape. A telegraph operator would then feed the tape into a transmitter, which would send the code across a cable network to its destination, where a stylus would press dots and dashes onto a paper ribbon for another operator to decode. (The irregular beeping sound of the code being transmitted became so familiar that many telegraph operators prided themselves on their ability to hear the dots and dashes and translate them into words.) The telegram would then be delivered like mail.

Unlike the telephone, which eventually became a household appliance, the telegraph was operated by specially trained staff and was usually part of the railroad system. To send a message, people would go to the nearest dispatch office or train station. Telegrams became a popular way to announce the birth of a baby or to send best wishes to be read at a wedding celebration.

he enrolled in a course offered by one of Samuel Morse's students. He finished with top marks and was immediately hired by the Montreal Telegraph Company to be a telegraph operator, one of the first in the country.

Gisborne soon saw the benefit of establishing a telegraph link between the Maritimes and the rest of Canada. Halifax was already a main port for mail and news dispatches arriving from Europe. Connecting that city by telegraph to central Canada would speed the travel of news. He went to New Brunswick and Nova Scotia in 1848 to persuade the governments there to support the building of telegraph lines. Nova Scotia was interested,

Did you know that the telegraph became an important means of putting down rebellion in the West? In the 1880s, a coast-to-coast network of telegraph lines was completed by the Canadian Pacific Railway. This was used during the 1885 Riel Rebellion by news reporters to send their stories back home and by the government to communicate with the North West Mounted Police.

Make a Telegraph

This easy-to-make telegraph uses a light to send Morse code signals. It could also be made with a buzzer, so you would hear it rather than see it. The supplies are available at any electronics store.

You will need:

- a battery holder (for 2 "C" batteries)
- 2 "C" batteries
- some plastic-coated wire
- wire strippers (or have an adult use a knife for this job)
- a small light socket (experimental type)
- a small bulb to fit the socket
- a push-button switch (momentary)

Making the Telegraph

1. Insert the bulb into the light socket and the batteries into the battery holder.
2. Connect one of the wires from the battery holder to a screw on the socket. Do this by loosening the screw, wrapping the bare wire around it, and tightening it up again. Connect the other wire to one of the metal prongs on the push-button switch.
3. Prepare a length of wire by cutting it to the size you want. Have an adult remove about 1/2 inch (1 cm) of plastic from each end using wire strippers or a knife.
4. Attach one end of the wire to the other screw on the socket and the other end to the second prong on the switch.
5. Press the button to make the bulb light up. Use the Morse code on page 49 to send out a simple message with long and short blinks of the light.

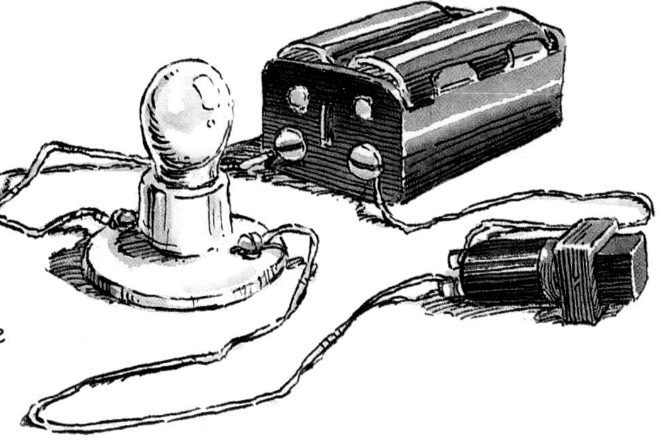

and by 1849 Gisborne was working for the Nova Scotia Telegraph Company. It was there that he began testing his ideas for laying cable under water. He knew that standard above-ground telegraph cable could not resist corrosion by salt water. A new kind of insulation was needed to protect it, and Gisborne experimented with various coatings to solve this problem.

Did you know that to get home from Nova Scotia in 1848, Gisborne snowshoed more than one hundred miles (160 km) while towing a toboggan loaded with about one hundred pounds (45 kg) of belongings and provisions? The British North American Telegraph Association gave him an award and a bonus to recognize this extraordinary effort.

A Transatlantic Dream

Eventually, Gisborne wanted to create a link between the easternmost point in North America (Newfoundland) and the westernmost point in the United Kingdom (Ireland). Not only was this the shortest route, but depth soundings indicated that there was a raised plateau along the ocean floor that extended from Newfoundland to Ireland. This would make it easier to lay the cable. To complete the line, another cable would have to connect Newfoundland to Nova Scotia. With a transatlantic cable as Gisborne envisioned it, Nova Scotia and Newfoundland would provide important communication links to the United States.

When it became clear that Gisborne was interested not only in connecting Nova Scotia to central Canada, but in establishing a two-thousand-mile (3,200 km) transatlantic cable, Nova Scotia's provincial secretary refused to allow him to raise money for the project, believing that it was a waste of time. So Gisborne and his new wife, Alida, moved to St. John's, Newfoundland. There he worked on building an overland telegraph from one end of the island to the other.

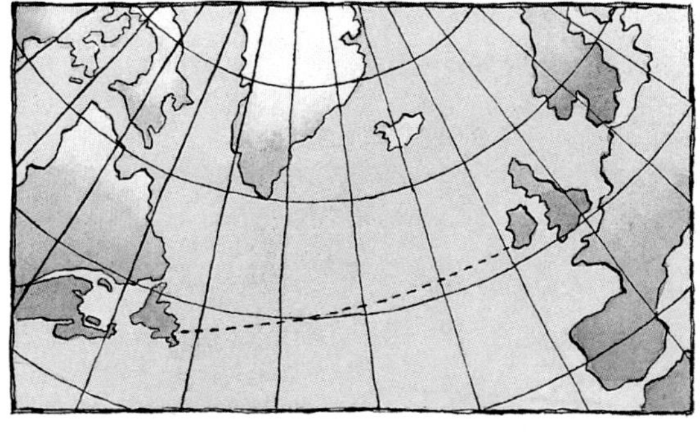

Anatomy of a Cable

The core of the cable was made up of a metal wire that conducted the signal and a rubber-like insulation designed to keep out salt water. The core was snugly wound in an "armor" made of lengths of wire wrapped in jute. At the shore end, the cable was given a heavier armor to protect it from the force of the tides and accidental damage by trawlers or ships' anchors.

Gisborne patented a formula for the armor and the insulation used in making submarine telegraph cables. His cable armor involved wrapping the outer wires around the core, half in one direction and half in the opposite direction, sometimes linking the two when they crossed. His cable insulation used several ingredients, but the main one was bituminous pitch (tar). This insulation was intended to protect the core from corrosion, but it also prevented rot and insect damage.

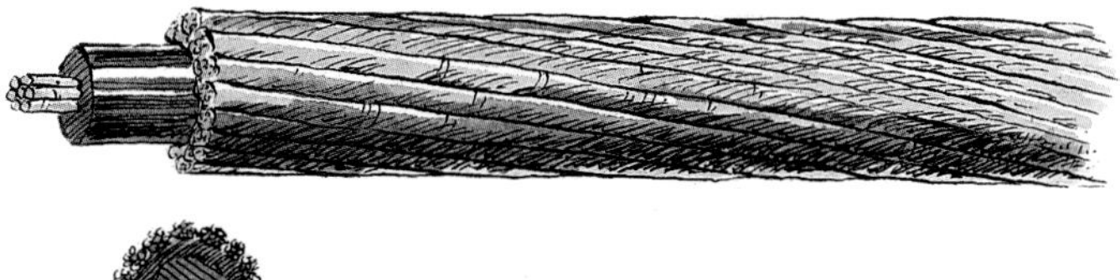

By 1856, Gisborne had found investors to back his transatlantic cable project, including the British engineer John Watkins Brett, who had successfully laid the world's first submarine cable. Because the Nova Scotia government was still being difficult, Gisborne stubbornly changed his route and planned to run the cable via Prince Edward Island and New Brunswick.

Of course, there was huge equipment to design before the link could be made, and Gisborne, eager to prove his ideas, began the engineering work. The ships that were to lay the cable would be outfitted with a reservoir, where the cable could be coiled around a spool. Above board, a series of large pulleys would allow the cable to be fed up from the hold to the stern and over. A braking system would ensure that the cable was lowered over the edge of the ship slowly and carefully, even while the vessel rocked on the waves, so the cable would not snap in two.

Gisborne invented the mechanisms for paying out the cable, ordered a cable to be manufactured in England, and successfully laid the first North American submarine cable between Prince Edward Island and New Brunswick in November 1852. Unlike Brett's submarine line, Gisborne's continued to work successfully for years.

Making the Dream a Reality

Gisborne's association with John Brett continued after the success of the Canadian undersea cable. The two men agreed to split the costs of laying the transatlantic cable between their two companies, and in 1853 the next part of the project, the laying of the overland line across Newfoundland from St. John's to Cape Ray, began.

Gisborne managed the crews of men hired to lay cable and build the road to Cape Ray. He ordered the necessary supplies, paid the bills and the wages of the workers, even arranged for provisions.

During the construction, a dispute broke out between the investors whose money was funding the venture. They backed out of the project and left Gisborne to pay the company's debts. He was forced to sell all of his property to cover the laborers' wages, and when he did not have enough to pay all his creditors, he was put in debtor's prison. The overland telegraph line across Newfoundland was left partially completed, and Gisborne's life was in ruin. Fortunately, influential friends eventually persuaded the government to release him from prison so that he could raise the funds needed to finish.

Brett continued to support the project, and he encouraged Gisborne to raise the remaining funds in North America. Early in 1854, Gisborne asked the American entrepreneur Cyrus Field to finance the venture. Field consulted with Samuel Morse to find out whether a transatlantic cable was realistic, and he discovered that Morse was very interested in the possibility. Encouraged, Field bought out Gisborne's company and acquired all the rights and privileges the government had originally granted him. Gisborne was hired as the chief engineer and began work on completing the land line across Newfoundland, but differences with Field soon led him to quit. Field's brother Matthew took charge of the project and completed the land line, spending extravagantly to do so.

Field was eager for a taste of success, so he gathered a number of society people on a ship to have a party and witness the laying of a cable from Newfoundland to Nova Scotia in 1855. Unfortunately, a storm came up and the cable had to be cut, leaving the partygoers disappointed and Field's investors wondering if the project was sensible after all. Gisborne was asked to return to the company as chief engineer, and the following year a submarine cable was successfully laid from Cape Ray, Newfoundland, to Cape Breton, Nova Scotia.

Plans continued for the laying of the transatlantic cable, but Gisborne left Field's company again in 1857, when he discovered that Field was conducting secret negotiations with Brett. Gisborne had lost control of the cable project, and he moved on to work in mining, where he patented inventions for drilling through rock and for detecting harmful gases in coal mines.

The Laying of the Transatlantic Cable

In 1857, Cyrus Field, together with Samuel Morse and Charles Bright, a British engineer and inventor, organized the first attempt to lay a transatlantic cable. The American ship *Niagara* and the British ship *Agamemnon* were to leave Ireland together, with the *Niagara* carrying the first half of the cable and the *Agamemnon* the second half. Only 325 miles (520 km) of cable had been payed out when an accident occurred. The cable had been feeding out too quickly, and when the brakes were applied to slow the process, the pressure was too much and the cable broke. Unfortunately, there was too little cable left to start over. The project had to wait until the following year.

Field arranged to have 250 miles (400 km) of extra cable on the 1858 expedition. A plan was developed so that if the cable had to be abandoned in a storm, the crew could return to the point where it had been left and continue the job later. The idea was to have reels of iron wire that could be attached to the end of the telegraph cable. In a storm, the telegraph cable would be cut and then carefully lowered to the bottom of the ocean; the iron wire would then be attached at the top end to a floating buoy marked with reflectors for the crew to find later. When the storm was over, they would locate the buoy and pull the cable up off the bottom with the help of the iron wire.

In 1858, the *Niagara* and the *Agamemnon* met in the middle of the ocean and spliced their cables together. Then the *Niagara* headed for Newfoundland and the *Agamemnon* for Ireland. On August 5 both ships arrived, and the first transatlantic cable was landed at Bay Bulls Arm in Trinity Bay, Newfoundland, and at Valencia, Ireland. The cable worked well, celebrations were held, and messages were exchanged between the president of the United States and Queen Victoria. Unfortunately, the cable worked for only four weeks before the insulation failed.

Did you know that in 1857, Cyrus Field argued with engineers who advised him not to rush the manufacture of the cable? To keep his American investors happy, he insisted that the cable be ready in June, which left only four months to do the job.

The American Civil War delayed further attempts until 1865, by which time telegraph technology had advanced. An enormous steamship called the *Great Eastern,* the largest ship in the world, was hired to lay the new transatlantic cable. In July 1865, the *Great Eastern* began the journey from Valencia to Heart's Content, Newfoundland, paying out the cable without difficulties until, only a day away from Newfoundland, it snapped. The public was beginning to lose faith in the dream of a transatlantic telegraph, but in 1866 a new cable was successfully landed at Heart's Content. The *Great Eastern* then returned to the place where the 1865 cable had snapped and retrieved it from the bottom of the ocean. The 1865 cable was spliced and brought to land at Heart's Content, where it worked just fine.

Did you know that telegraph systems became an essential military tool for managing troops? In the 1890s the British, concerned that the Atlantic cables were controlled by private American interests, began exploring strategies for ensuring government access to telegraph communications in the event that Britain went to war with the United States. An "all-British" Pacific cable was finally laid in 1902, linking Australia to British Columbia.

Chapter 5

Sending Sound Across Wires by Telephone

On the night of March 10, 1876, in a Boston attic, Alexander Graham Bell and Thomas Watson prepared to do another experiment on the new device they were working on. Bell had been granted a patent for a "telephone," but so far the two men had had little luck sending sound through the wires that weaved between two rooms. Tonight, they would try again.

Watson left Bell in front of the **transmitter** and went to sit in front of the **receiver**. Suddenly, Bell spilled sulfuric acid on himself. The acid began burning a hole in his trousers, and Bell shouted, "Mr. Watson, come here, I want you!" Watson heard Bell's call for help on the receiver and raced to him. When he ran through the door, he stopped. The two men stared at each other. Then they whooped happily and began laughing and crying at the same time. They had just made the first telephone call! They were so excited that they forgot all about the spilled acid, and spent the whole night talking on the telephone.

Bell's Early Years

Alexander Graham Bell was born on March 3, 1847, in Edinburgh, Scotland, into a family concerned with sound and communication. Both his father and his grandfather were speech teachers. In fact, his father, Alexander Melville Bell, had invented Visible Speech, a system of communication that uses written symbols to represent sounds. It was used to correct speech defects and to teach deaf people how to speak. Alexander Graham Bell and his two brothers became speech teachers too. In the late 1860s, however, both of Bell's brothers died of tuberculosis. Then Alexander became ill. Not wanting to lose their only remaining child, Bell's parents decided to move to North America, where the climate would be healthier. In 1870, they immigrated to Tutela Heights, just outside Brantford, Ontario.

Within a year and a half, Bell had recovered enough to take a teaching position at a school for the deaf in Boston. He used Visible Speech, and explained to his students that vibrations made by speaking produce sound waves. These sound waves travel through the air and then turn back into vibrations in the ear of the person hearing the sound. He thought up all sorts of ways to demonstrate this to his students, even having them feel his neck and face when he made a sound and then copy the feeling themselves. He was a kind and patient teacher, and he found that students worked better when he encouraged them.

Bell taught all day and experimented at night. He was particularly interested in inventing a multiple (or harmonic) telegraph. The existing telegraph system was slow and could carry only two messages at the same time, one outgoing and one incoming. But a

Reading and Writing by Touch

Several years before Bell's father invented Visible Speech, Louis Braille, an eleven-year-old student at the National Institute for Blind Children in Paris, France, devised a way to make it easier for blind people to communicate. He invented a code of raised dots that would allow them to read and write by touch. He got the idea from a military code used in night communications. Soldiers could use it to send and receive messages after dark without revealing their position by lighting lamps. Braille simplified the military code, and assigned the dots to letters, numbers, and punctuation marks, instead of sounds. Braille and his friends taught themselves the system by sending notes back and forth to each other at the institute, where they also lived. Over nine years, Braille experimented and improved his system. His invention eventually became the worldwide written communication system for the blind.

The Native Warrior

While Bell was recovering from his illness at home near Brantford, he became friends with several Mohawk who lived in the area. He studied the Mohawk language and culture, and translated Mohawk into Visible Speech. The tribe honored him by making him an honorary chief and teaching him their war dance. For the rest of his life, Bell did the war dance or shouted out war cries whenever he felt very happy or excited.

Did you know that Bell's mother was deaf? She used an ear trumpet, an old-fashioned hearing aid, and felt the vibrations of sounds around her. When Bell played the piano, his mother would put her hand on the instrument to feel the music.

multiple telegraph would be able to send many messages in each direction at the same time. Bell planned to base his invention on the principle of **resonance**. As a pianist, he knew that when one tuning fork is struck, another one of the same note (with the same **frequency**) resonates. This means it vibrates at the same speed and produces the same sound as the first tuning fork. He also knew that each note created a different electrical current through a wire, and that if identical groups of tuning forks were placed at the sending and receiving ends of that wire, only the matching tuning fork would register the message (or note), so messages could not be scrambled.

In 1872, Bell decided to give private lessons instead of teaching at schools. His first pupil was five-year-old George Sanders. George and his nurse took rooms in Bell's boardinghouse, and when George's father, Thomas Sanders, visited, he saw the wires Bell had strung up and the equipment he had made. He became interested in Bell's experiments, and the next year Bell moved in with the Sanders family. In exchange for teaching George, Bell received free room and board, and had the entire basement to devote to his experiments. He taught at Boston University, worked with George, and experimented at night. He also took on some other private pupils, including a young woman named Mabel Hubbard.

Did you know that although Bell is famous for inventing the telephone, he considered teaching the deaf to be his most important accomplishment?

One Sunday afternoon, while visiting Mabel's family in Boston, Bell told her father, Gardiner Green Hubbard, about his idea for a multiple telegraph. Hubbard liked Bell's idea and offered him financial backing. When Bell told him that Thomas Sanders had already offered to invest, Hubbard replied that it would be good to have more than one person supplying money. He urged Bell to suggest that the men divide ownership in the invention three ways. Sanders agreed, and the three became business partners. Hubbard and Sanders would provide the finances, and Bell would invent the apparatus.

Finally, Bell had enough money to pay someone else to build the equipment he needed. Although he knew what he wanted and could design the pieces, he was not as good at building them. So he went to the Charles Williams Electrical Shop in Boston and submitted his design for a transmitter and a receiver for his multiple telegraph. Thomas Watson was assigned to build it. When Bell picked up the finished pieces, he noticed a small mistake and spoke to Watson about it. The two men liked each other, and Bell asked Watson if he wanted to assist him with his experiments. Watson answered an enthusiastic yes, and the two men would work together for many years.

An Idea Occurs

Every summer, Bell returned home to Brantford, where he continued his experiments and discussed them with his father. During the summer of 1874, he was working on his ideas for the multiple telegraph when an idea struck him. If code could be sent across wires using electrical pulses, why couldn't sound? If an electric current varies in intensity in response to sound, it ought to be possible to telegraph *any* sound. The possibility excited him.

Bell had always been involved in the science of *making* sound, but now he needed to teach himself about *hearing* sound. He had a doctor friend send him a real human ear to study, and he observed that a tiny, thin membrane is what moves the ear bones and receives sound. He thought that something much larger and stronger could work as a membrane to send sound through wires, and he began experimenting with this idea in his parents' barn. His father used to jokingly tell people that his son was out in the barn trying to send sound through cans and wires. At the time, this idea sounded crazy.

At the end of the summer, Bell returned to teaching and experimenting in Boston. When he arrived, he told Watson about his idea and sketched the equipment he thought he needed. He even had a name for his new machine: telephone, from the Greek words *tele* (meaning "afar off") and *phone* (meaning "sound").

In March 1875, Bell met with Joseph Henry, a famous physicist, at the Smithsonian Institution. Bell had made many discoveries during his experiments, and he wanted to know which ones were really new and which ones other people had already found. He knew Professor Henry could tell him. They first discussed Bell's telegraphy experiments, then Bell told Henry about his idea for a telephone. When he explained that he didn't have the electrical knowledge necessary to develop the apparatus, Henry said, "Get it!" This idea was so exciting that the professor thought Bell should develop it himself.

Make Your Own Telephone

Bell's father used to tease his son about trying to send sound through wires and tin cans, but Bell knew it could be done. You can imitate his experiments by making your own simple telephone.

You will need:

- 2 clean, same-sized tin cans with no sharp edges and one open end (or 2 strong, clean plastic cups)
- a nail
- a hammer
- 2 paper clips
- string (at least 3 feet [90 cm] long)

Making the Phone

Place each can or cup with the mouth down. Using the hammer and nail, pierce a small hole in the center of the top end of the cans, then thread the string through the holes in each one. Tie each end of string to a paper clip. This will hold the string in place so it doesn't slip out the hole.

You and a friend each take one can or cup. Move far enough apart to pull the string tight. Each can or cup is both the mouthpiece and the earpiece, so one of you listens while the other one speaks. To test your telephone, one of you should read messages into one end while the other writes down what he or she hears at the other end. See how many messages get through correctly.

What's happening? When one of you speaks into your can or cup, it and the string pick up the sound vibrations. These travel along the string to the other can or cup, where the listener hears the speaker's voice. If you try to use your telephone when the string is loose, the sound will stop.

Experiment with different sizes of cans or cups (it works better if both are always the same size). You can tie more string and additional cans to the main string so three or more of you can carry on a conversation together.

Did you know that the first telephones used the same piece for speaking and hearing? After you spoke, you turned your head and put your ear to the mouthpiece to hear the person at the other end respond.

By then, Bell and Watson were doing experiments in the attic of the shop where Watson worked. For months, they tested tuning forks, wires, batteries, electromagnets, and more. One night, they were using organ reeds and one got stuck. Watson, who was in the room with the transmitter, plucked the reed with his finger. In the other room, Bell, who was with the receiver, heard a twang. This was their breakthrough – they knew at once that Bell's idea was possible.

The key to the telephone would be an unbroken current that varies in intensity much as air density varies with different sounds. Bell called this a continuous undulatory current. It differs from the stop-and-start current used to send telegraph code. Bell sketched an idea for equipment, and Watson built it the next day. Then Watson strung wires from the attic to his workbench two floors below. When the men tested their apparatus the next night, it didn't work. But they weren't discouraged, because they knew they were on the right track. Determinedly, they continued experimenting. By June 1875, Bell had converted his ideas into a scientific basis for the telephone.

When Bell told Gardiner Hubbard about his experiments with the telephone, he wasn't interested. He and Thomas Sanders knew that the multiple telegraph would make a lot of money, and they thought Bell was wasting his time on the telephone. By this time, Bell and Mabel Hubbard had fallen in love and wanted to marry. But Mabel's father told Bell that if he kept teaching and working on the telephone, he would not be allowed to marry his daughter. Bell was upset but stubborn. He decided that if Mabel loved him, she'd understand how important these things were to him. Meanwhile, Mabel discovered her father's threat. When Bell visited the Hubbards that week, Mabel was so angry with her father that she told Bell she loved him and would "be engaged to him that very day." And she encouraged him to keep working on the telephone.

The First Telephone

Eventually, Gardiner Hubbard accepted Bell and Mabel's engagement. And though he still didn't believe the telephone had any future, he encouraged Bell to apply for a patent for it. The patent was granted on March 3, 1876. By this time, Bell and Watson had moved into the same boardinghouse in Boston to make it easier to conduct their experiments at night. One week after receiving the patent, they made the first telephone call with an improved transmitter that Bell had designed and Watson had built. All night long, they took turns at the transmitter and the receiver, just saying, "One, two, three, four . . ." when they couldn't think of anything else. And the last words that night were Bell's shout of "God save the Queen!"

Did you know that Thomas Watson invented the telephone's ring? The first telephones had no way to signal that someone was calling. Watson tried a buzzer and then a device that thumped, but they weren't very effective. When he thought of the name of the inventor, he put in a bell.

The first telephone sent messages only one way. It was composed of three main parts: a transmitter for sending a message, a receiver for hearing it, and a wire connecting them together. When someone spoke into the transmitter, a flexible metal **diaphragm** vibrated in a field produced by a magnet. A wire attached to the diaphragm moved up and down in a metal cup that held a mixture of sulfuric acid and water. This produced an electric current that changed with the different vibrations and traveled through the wire to the receiver. At the receiver, the current went into another magnetic field, which made another diaphragm vibrate, and thus the original sounds were reproduced.

Now that Bell had a working telephone, people needed to see it. Mabel urged him to enter both it and the harmonic telegraph in Philadelphia's Centennial Exposition in 1876.

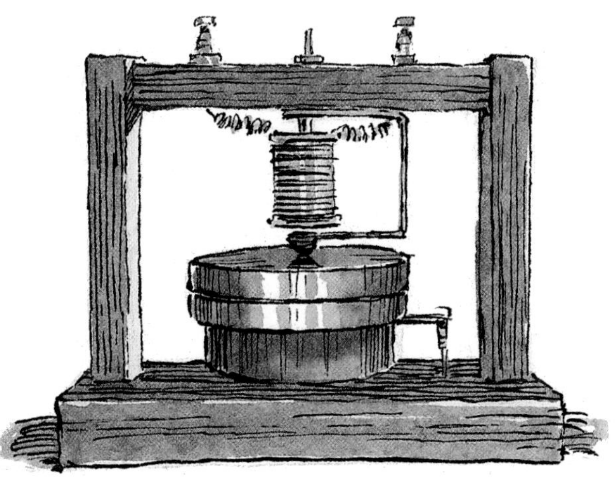

Initially, Bell refused, saying that the telephone needed more work before he would show it, but Mabel pressured him. When he argued with her, she just closed her eyes and told him that she couldn't see anything he was saying. Finally, he gave in. Then the date for judging the exhibits was changed and Bell again refused to go. With her mother, Mabel devised a plan. The two women arrived at Bell's school in Boston and took him for an afternoon drive – to the train station. Mabel gave him a ticket to Philadelphia and a bag she'd packed with some of his clothes. When Bell still refused to leave, she told him that she wouldn't marry him if he didn't go. Bell got on the train.

On June 25, 1876, the judges at the exposition were to come and see Bell's invention. But it was a very hot day, and the judges grew tired quickly. They decided to stop at the table before Bell's. Fortunately, Dom Pedro, the emperor of Brazil, recognized Bell (whom he'd met once in Boston) and asked about his display. When Bell told him about the telephone, Dom Pedro insisted that the judges try it. He went to the receiver, which was in another part of the hall, and listened while the judges stayed with Bell, who spoke into the transmitter. When Dom Pedro heard Bell reciting Shakespeare, he dropped the receiver and shouted, "My God! It speaks!" Impressed, all the judges took turns listening and speaking into the telephone. They tested the wires and equipment, and they even moved the receiver down one floor to make sure no trickery was involved. They went from being hot and tired to excitedly spending three hours talking on the telephone. The next day, the telephone was moved to the Judges' Hall and Bell won an award for both the telephone and the harmonic telegraph.

Did you know that people at Philadelphia's Centennial Exposition made so much noise about Bell's telephone that the police came rushing over to see if the hall was on fire?

Putting It to the Test

Bell knew that his next challenge was to make sure that the telephone worked across distance. As usual, he spent the summer near Brantford with his family, and soon he had made the first long-distance telephone calls.

Wires connected the Bell house with the barn, and Bell tested the telephone every day, often with the help of neighbors. Finally, he felt ready. He arranged with the local telegraph company to use its wires between Brantford and Mount Pleasant, Ontario, a five-mile (8 km) distance, on August 3, 1876.

That evening, a nervous Alexander Graham Bell took his receiver to a telegraph office in Mount Pleasant. Word had spread about his experiment, and people gathered to see what would happen. At the right time, Bell held the receiver to his ear and crossed his fingers. The words "To be or not to be" came crackling through the receiver, but there was a lot of static. The telegraph operator sent a message in Morse code to Brantford to have them switch to high-resistance coils. Again, Bell nervously put the receiver to his ear. "To be or not to be," repeated his uncle David. This time, the message was clear. Bell was relieved and excited – and so were the people watching the experiment. In Brantford, people took turns talking and singing into the telephone while the telegraph operator in Mount Pleasant kept sending messages that their voices were coming through.

The most famous call almost did not happen. Bell had written to the Dominion Telegraph Company in Toronto, asking to rent the telegraph line between Brantford and Paris, Ontario, for one hour on August 10, 1876. But the person who received the letter did not take it seriously and threw it in the garbage. Fortunately, an assistant named Lewis B. McFarlane recognized Bell's name. He fished the letter out of the trash and arranged to let Bell use the lines. Because the

telegraph company had not replied to Bell's request, however, everyone assumed that the call was not going to happen and his father left for a meeting out of town. But at the last minute, a letter arrived giving Bell the permission he needed. He grabbed his equipment and rushed to get to Paris, eight miles (13 km) away, in time to receive the messages from Brantford.

When Bell got there, the Paris office was full of people, with others waiting on the street outside. At eight o'clock, he raised the receiver to his ear. He was nervous because the power for this call was coming from a battery sixty-eight miles (110 km) away in Toronto. But then he heard a voice. Everyone exclaimed in amazement. Suddenly, Bell told the telegraph operator to ask if he was hearing his father's voice. "Yes," his father said into the telephone. He had not wanted to miss this important event for his son, so he had turned back and missed his meeting instead.

Success at Last

When Bell returned to Boston in the autumn, he hired Thomas Watson as his full-time assistant. Hubbard still wanted Bell to concentrate on the multiple telegraph, but Mabel encouraged him to keep working on the telephone as well. She also encouraged him to do "telephonic lectures" to earn some money from the invention. Bell would travel to different cities with his telephone receivers while Watson stayed in Boston with the transmitter. People would gather in auditoriums where speakers were set up, hear Bell explain his invention, then listen to Watson speak and sing to them from far away. With his first earnings, Bell had a tiny silver model of the

Home on Cape Breton Island

During the summer of 1885, the Bells traveled to Baddeck, on Cape Breton Island in Nova Scotia. It reminded Bell of his early home in Scotland, and he wanted to live there. For years after, the Bell family spent half a year in the U.S. and the other half at Baddeck, and Bell had laboratories at both places. In 1892, the Bells built a mansion at Baddeck and called it Beinn Bhreagh (Gaelic for "beautiful mountain").

At Baddeck, friends and neighbors took part in Bell's many experiments. In fact, many Cape Bretoners associate him more with his other inventions, which included flying machines, a vacuum jacket to help patients breathe artificially, a metal detector, an electric probe that could detect bullets in a body so surgeons could remove them, a foghorn for submarines, a hydrofoil, and the photophone.

On August 2, 1922, Alexander Graham Bell died at Beinn Bhreagh while holding Mabel's hand. He is buried there, at the top of his "beautiful mountain," and Mabel Hubbard Bell, who died shortly afterward, is buried beside him.

Did you know that Bell considered the telephone to be a nuisance? When he walked in to his laboratory, he would wrap a towel around it to muffle it and say, "Now a man can think."

telephone made for Mabel. It's ironic that the woman who played such a role in the invention of the telephone was deaf.

Some people claimed that the telephone was just a fad and predicted that the excitement it generated would fizzle out quickly. However, its popularity steadily increased. Hubbard and Sanders, who had been interested only in the multiple telegraph, initially refused to take any money earned from the telephone. But Bell insisted that they were all partners, and eventually the three men became very wealthy.

On July 9, 1877, Alexander Graham Bell, Thomas Watson, Gardiner Hubbard, and Thomas Sanders founded the Bell Telephone Company. Bell still hated having to deal with finances, so when he and Mabel married on July 11, he gave her all the rights in his new company and all but ten of his shares as a wedding present.

Soon people realized the value of the patent for the telephone, and they began challenging Bell's ownership of it. Companies filed lawsuits claiming that other people, including Elisha Gray and Thomas Edison, were the real inventors. Most simply wanted to cancel Bell's patents and take advantage of the technology themselves. Eventually, Bell was spending so much time and money defending himself that he could not devote himself to his school and it closed.

Although Bell won every lawsuit, companies continued to challenge him, even after the United States Supreme Court ruled that he was the one and only inventor of the telephone, and that his method of using electricity to send speech over wires was the only known way to do it. In all, Bell spent almost twenty years fighting various lawsuits. But the patent for the telephone proved to be the single most valuable one in history.

On January 25, 1915, Alexander Graham Bell sat in front of a telephone in New York City while Thomas Watson waited by one in San Francisco. They were about to place the first telephone call across the United States. Officials gave Bell messages that they had written for him to say, but instead he picked up the phone and called, "Hoy, hoy, Mr. Watson! Mr. Watson, come here, I want you!" And Watson gleefully replied, "I'd like to, Dr. Bell, but this time it would take me a week!"

Did you know that Bell answered the telephone with the words "Hoy! Hoy!" instead of "Hello" because he thought it sounded better?

Chapter 6

Wireless Finds a Voice: Fessenden and the Modern Radio

As soon as Bell invented the telephone, a ten-year-old boy named Reg started clipping every newspaper article he could find about it. Because Reg lived in Fergus, Ontario, which was not far from Bell's home of Brantford, news of the telephone was in all the papers. His clippings soon filled a scrapbook. That summer of 1876, the young boy discussed Bell's invention with his uncle Cortez Fessenden, who was a physics and math teacher. Reg wanted to know why Bell needed wires to send his voice if a clap of thunder could travel great distances without any wires at all. Cortez was sure there was some scientific explanation, but even with his knowledge of physics, he could not answer this riddle.

Finding the solution to this puzzle became Reginald Fessenden's main goal. Ten years later, Fessenden asked the great inventor Thomas Edison, for whom he was working in New York, what the chances were of sending speech without wires. Edison replied, "Fezzy, what do you say are man's chances of jumping over the moon? I figure that one is about as likely as the other."

Did you know that Reg was home-schooled until he was nine? When his mother found him running a toy snowplow with parts from his father's clock, she assigned him more Latin verbs to study, hoping to keep him out of mischief. Reg had for some time been removing the clock parts early in the week and using them to motorize his toy. Later in the week, he would reassemble the clock – just in time for his father, an Anglican priest, to calculate the length of his sermon for Sunday morning.

Laying the Groundwork

Before Fessenden could solve his riddle, he knew he would need to understand more about electricity. In 1886, there was still much to be learned about the mysterious waves that would become the key to radio communication.

Did you know that Reg's first experiment resulted in snowballs in June? He packed snow into a box, covered it with boughs, and stashed it along the banks of the Grand River in Fergus, keeping track of the daily temperature in a notebook. On a hot June day, he surprised his friends by starting a snowball fight.

Twenty years earlier, James Clerk Maxwell had theorized that these waves, called **electromagnetic waves**, could travel through the air and be picked up at a distance. Heinrich Hertz's experiments in the 1880s proved that Maxwell was correct.

Even though so much was still a mystery, Fessenden believed that the study of electricity was where he would probably find the answers to his riddle about sending speech without wires. So his first task was to learn everything he could about this new science. He had the chance to do this while helping Edison solve a serious problem with the electrical wires he had developed to run his lighting systems. The wires were catching fire because the rubber insulation that was wrapped around them was **flammable**. Edison needed to find a new kind of casing for his wires, one that would bend easily and could stand up to the heat produced by the electric current. Without new, safer electrical wiring, Edison knew he would have difficulty selling his lighting products to the wary public.

Fessenden began by trying to understand what makes rubber catch fire and what makes it elastic. Rather than following other people's ideas, he experimented on his own. He spent twenty-four hours a day in the lab, testing hundreds of compounds, and eventually concluded that rubber was flammable because it contained too many hydrogen atoms. His solution was to find a way of replacing the hydrogen atoms with more stable chlorine atoms, which would give him a compound that did not burn.

Having solved the problem of flammability,

Did you know that when Fessenden needed a rest during his long days in the lab, he would take a nap on the floor with Watt's Chemical Dictionary for a pillow?

Fessenden needed to find out how to make the new coverings flexible like the old rubber ones had been. To start, he decided to examine all the known qualities of the elements from the periodic table. He wrote down all the elements on slips of paper, arranged them in order, and compared all of their descriptive qualities (their size, volume, weight, and so on). He found that there was a complex pattern that determined rigidity or elasticity.

Fessenden also discovered something that everyone now learns in science class: atoms have a positive core, and a negative electrical charge surrounds the core. He called this the electrostatic doublet theory. As a result of his study of the elements, Fessenden concluded that it was the particular kind of electrical attraction between the molecules that held them together and made rubber flexible. He tested his theory on a number of metals and found his calculations came out right.

In 1892, Fessenden wrote a paper explaining that molecules are attracted to each other because of the way these electrical charges work. This was not the accepted theory at the time. It was commonly believed that gravity, not electricity, held things together, and therefore it was also believed that gravity made rubber elastic. Even the great physicist Lord Kelvin had said, "Obviously, the fact that rubber particles stick together cannot possibly be due to electricity. Every physicist knows that it is because of gravitation." As it turned out, Fessenden was right, although it would be many years before scientists agreed with his findings.

Now that Fessenden understood elasticity, it was a simple matter for him to develop a compound that would satisfy Edison's need for a better covering for his wires. His work for Edison also taught him to practice solving complex scientific problems by going back to basics, or what he called first principles – just as he did when he started with the periodic table and compared each of the elements. Fessenden was not afraid to question established theories. In fact, he made a point of examining them with skepticism. His stubborn and creative personality was a key to his later efforts to invent voice radio, an undertaking that would set him in direct opposition to Edison and Italy's Guglielmo Marconi.

The Beginnings of Wireless

The dream of transmitting voice without wires came one step closer to reality when, in 1888, Heinrich Hertz found a way to send electromagnetic waves through the air from a transmitter to a receiver. Hertz's signals did not travel along wire as telegraph and telephone messages do, so his experiments were the beginning of what was initially called wireless and later became known as radio. His work paved the way for many inventors who followed, including Marconi and Fessenden.

Hertz's transmitter, called an electric spark generator, was used in early wireless telegraphy.

In 1896, Marconi first succeeded in sending telegraph signals by wireless. He was making great strides in improving his system, and was getting a lot of public attention. His apparatus allowed messages to be sent in Morse code without using a telegraph cable. This was a major achievement. It meant that for the first time, there could be communication between a ship at sea and a wireless telegraph station on land.

Did you know that in 1898, during a yachting regatta, Marconi's wireless system was installed on a tugboat so journalists could transmit the results of the races to shore? This feat of communication, the first commercial transmission from sea to shore, was front-page news and prompted Queen Victoria to have a Marconi wireless link installed between her residence on the Isle of Wight and the royal yacht, where her son was getting over a broken knee.

Unlike Marconi, Fessenden wanted to invent a system that would support both the dots and dashes of wireless telegraphy and the voice messages of wireless telephony; sending speech without wires was still his dream. Transmitting radio messages involved sending signals out through the air from a transmitter to a receiver, where the signals were captured

Send a Friend Secret Messages

Before Fessenden invented AM radio, all radio messages were sent in Morse code. The short and long signals were called "dits" and "dahs" because of the sound they made on the telegraph. Using the code below, try to send messages to a friend. You can also build the telegraph on page 29 with an extra-long wire and send your messages into another room.

A	. —	M	— —	Y	— . — —
B	— . . .	N	— .	Z	— — . .
C	— . — .	O	— — —	1	. — — — —
D	— . .	P	. — — .	2	. . — — —
E	.	Q	— — . —	3	. . . — —
F	. . — .	R	. — .	4	. . . . —
G	— — .	S	. . .	5	. . . . .
H	. . . .	T	—	6	— . . . .
I	. .	U	. . —	7	— — . . .
J	. — — —	V	. . . —	8	— — — . .
K	— . —	W	. — —	9	— — — — .
L	. — . .	X	— . . —	10	— — — — —

and decoded. Fessenden was frustrated, however, with the existing type of radio-wave detector, called a **coherer**, which he felt could never do a good enough job to pick up voice messages. The coherer had a glass tube filled with carbon filings that linked together in a fuzzy line when a radio signal was detected. For the device to be able to receive the next part of a message, a small hammer-like tool had to tap on the glass tube and shake the carbon filings loose again. The coherer was fine for the intermittent Morse code signals Marconi was sending, but it would never be able to cope with the continuous signals of Fessenden's voice radio.

For Fessenden, this was a discouraging time when there seemed little hope of progress with his research. So during the summer of 1897, he took some time off from his work in Pittsburgh as a professor of electrical engineering to visit his uncle Cortez at a cottage near Peterborough, Ontario. Fessenden had been hearing a lot of discussion about the Marconi wireless and the "whiplash" method of sending Hertzian waves (a method that used a stop-and-go pulse that we would now call a digital signal). During that summer spent under the trees at the lake, Fessenden came to the realization that in order to transmit voice, the Hertzian signals would have to move continuously. He compared it to the waves that ripple outward from a stone tossed in a lake. The stop-and-go signal of the existing wireless, he now understood, would not do the job. Marconi was on the wrong track.

The Long Road to Success

The journey from idea to reality was a difficult one. One day, while experimenting back in Pittsburgh, Fessenden was working with a device called an **interrupter**. He used the interrupter

Did you know that it was radio telegraphy that sent the distress call from the Titanic and brought the rescue ship that saved 700 of the 2,200 passengers?

with spark transmitters to send the stop-and-go signals Marconi was using. In another room, his assistant was sending Morse code and got the telegraph key stuck. When Fessenden put on his headphones, expecting to hear the click-clack of the Morse code, he was amazed to hear instead the squeal of the interrupter itself: he was finally sending a sound, not just the pulses of code. This was his first glimmer of success, and Fessenden began to work furiously on improvements to his equipment. He had an opportunity to do this in a new job with the U.S. government.

In 1900, Fessenden's telegraph system secured him work with the U.S. Weather Bureau. They needed a way to send weather reports more quickly along the Atlantic coast, and Fessenden convinced them that his equipment could do the job, and that certain improvements, such as a more powerful generator, would make the system useful for weather forecasting. A lot of shipping occurred along the Atlantic seaboard, but so did hurricanes and other weather systems that threatened the crews and cargo traveling from port to port. The shipping companies needed fast and accurate information about the conditions offshore to avoid losses of life and property.

Fessenden, his wife, Helen, and their son, Ken, moved to Cobb Island, Maryland, where he set up a telegraph station. The Weather Bureau did not want him wasting taxpayers' money on the foolish idea of sending voice messages, so Fessenden concentrated on delivering telegraph services. But whenever his telegraph work was done for the day, he would turn to his own experiments, making improvements that would allow his equipment to handle voice signals (telephony) as well as telegraphy.

Many different pieces of equipment make up a radio system, and Fessenden experimented with them all, making improvements and taking out patents for his various inventions. In September 1900, he had a new interrupter made, one that could break the current ten thousand times per second, and by December 1900, Fessenden was finally ready to try out this new device.

On Cobb Island, there were two fifty-foot (15 m) towers one mile (1.6 km) apart. Using one tower to transmit and the other to receive, Fessenden wanted to try sending a voice message. His assistant, Alfred Thiesson, listened at his end for the transmission, but at first he got only noise. Fessenden checked his calculations but could find no errors; in his frustration, he turned off his equipment. What could be the problem? It made no sense. He then turned on the steam engine that ran his generator, wanting to run through everything one more time. When the engine started up the second time, he noticed that it was running faster than before. All the connections were fine, so he tried his message again: "One, two, three, four. Is it snowing where you are, Mr. Thiesson? If so, telegraph back and let me know." Thiesson frantically telegraphed back that he had heard the words

Messages Across the Miles: From Telegraph to Radio

Telegraphy: Morse code sent through wires (Samuel Morse, 1845)
Telephony: Voice sent through wires (Alexander Graham Bell, 1876)
Radio Telegraphy: Morse code sent on radio waves with no wires (Guglielmo Marconi, 1896)
Radio Telephony: Voice sent on radio waves with no wires (Reginald Fessenden, 1900)

a mile away. The first wireless voice transmission was made that day, December 23, 1900.

This was the beginning of radio as we know it today, but Fessenden would face many more trials before the world knew about his success. The year 1902 was his most productive and disastrous one yet. What some consider his most significant contribution to the development of radio came that year, but he also found himself in grave financial difficulty. (He left the Weather Bureau when his boss tried to take partial credit for his inventions.)

It was during this tumultuous year that he developed and named the **heterodyne principle**, which is still the foundation of modern radio communication. Heterodyning is a process of detecting an incoming signal by beating a second radio wave against it, thus producing a third wave. The result is a signal that can be heard by the human ear.

Did you know that Fessenden's work for the Weather Bureau occasionally took him to Roanoke Island, North Carolina? While there, he got to know the Wright brothers, who were experimenting with gliders a few miles away. They finally took flight in one in 1902, not long after Fessenden left his job with the government.

Fessenden based this idea on something he had noticed when playing notes on a piano. When the two notes C and B were played separately, they each had their own sound frequency. When they were played together, however, a third frequency was created. The heterodyne principle accomplished the same thing using radio waves.

"We Are Getting You, Brant Rock, Loud and Clear"

Without his job at the Weather Bureau, Fessenden needed to find a new way to finance his research. In 1905, two wealthy businessmen from Pittsburgh, T. H. Given and Hay Walker, agreed to form the National Electric Signaling Company with him. Fessenden set up a telegraph station at Brant Rock, near Boston, and hired assistants to work with him on improving his telegraph system.

Marconi had made a big splash in the newspapers when he successfully transmitted a signal across the Atlantic in 1901, and Fessenden wanted to see if his system could do the same. He sent his best engineer, James Armor, to a

station he ha[…]
that all the s[…]
in January 19[…]
message out a[…]
Morse code w[…]
soon received […]
you, Brant Ro[…]
month, Fessen[…]
transatlantic w[…]

Fessenden h[…]
for creating his […]
best equipment […]
was a **high-frequency alternator**. Over the years, he had experimented with this kind of equipment, but he decided that he needed a model that was more powerful and operated at a higher frequency than was ever heard of before, about 100 kilohertz (kHz). He wrote up the specifications and placed an order for the alternator, but the one that was made would give only 10 kHz. When he stripped it […]nd rebuilt it, he was able to get 70 […]od enough for a start.

[…] fall of 1906, after his transatlantic […] Fessenden was testing this new high-[…]y alternator. A surprise awaited him. […]nber, Armor, who was still working […]nd, sent a registered letter saying that […]was working on the telegraph one […]d heard the voice of Adam Stein, […]senden's assistants back at Brant […]ead of the dots and dashes of Morse […] voice had been transmitted across the Atlantic to Scotland without wires!

Fessenden was eager to give a demonstration of voice radio, but his plans were dashed when a winter storm destroyed the radio tower in Scotland. He had to find another way to present his findings, so he decided to take advantage of the many ships that traveled up and down the Atlantic coastline, particularly those belonging to the U.S. Navy and the United Fruit Company, which had on board the Fessenden wireless system. Always a man who enjoyed a celebration, he planned a special Christmas Eve broadcast, the first in history.

On December 24, 1906, Fessenden's radio broadcast was heard up and down the Atlantic coast by crews onboard ship. They had been warned to be ready for an unusual message on Christmas Eve, but the sailors couldn't believe their ears when they heard a short voice message from Reginald Fessenden, followed by Handel's *Largo* played on Edison's phonograph. The program finished with Fessenden playing "O Holy Night" on the violin and singing

Did you know that Fessenden's constant companion at Brant Rock was a cat called Mikkums? He rescued this half-drowned kitten, then rubbed it all over with butter to encourage it to clean its fur and get warm. No sooner was the butter finished than the kitten curled up in the coal scuttle and needed a real bath!

the last verse. Mail flooded in from astonished people who had heard the broadcast.

The broadcast was repeated on New Year's Eve, and was heard as far away as the Caribbean. Fessenden was not surprised that so many people had been able to hear it, because he knew that his radio detector was being used illegally by many wireless systems. He wrote, "As a matter of fact, at the time of the broadcast, practically everyone was infringing on the liquid **barretter**. When the broadcast was made, practically every ship along the coast was equipped to receive it."

The successes of 1906 should have led to fame and financial success for Fessenden, but Given and Walker had their own ideas about the future direction of the National Electric Signaling Company. They tricked Fessenden and took control of his patents. Others used his inventions without paying for the right to do so, and he spent many years and thousands of dollars defending himself and his patents in court. In the end, he won a settlement of $500,000 for his invention of radio, far less than it was worth, but enough to pay his legal expenses and allow him to retire with his wife. By this time, other people's names were being connected with radio, and Fessenden was forgotten as the new industry grew and became a familiar part of everyday life.

Did you know that when Fessenden demonstrated his voice radio equipment in December 1906, Scientific American magazine wrote that the sound quality was better than that of the telephone? His broadcast was clear and easy to hear, with no interference noise, proving that his inventions had advanced radio science by a huge step.

Fessenden's Other Inventions

After the sinking of the *Titanic* in 1912, there was general concern about safety at sea. How could an iceberg, such as the one struck by the *Titanic*, be detected in time to avoid a crash? Fessenden invented the fathometer to solve this problem, and thus radically changed the world of marine travel. He found that he was able to detect objects by listening to echoes transmitted by an underwater microphone. When placed aboard a ship, this device told the captain exactly how deep the water was and whether there were obstacles in the ship's path. The fathometer won Fessenden the Scientific American Gold Medal.

Fessenden also experimented with photography, which he found a useful way to collect and preserve information. He foresaw the need to store information in a newer, more compact form than books, and invented a system of microfilm. He imagined the treasures of the British Museum, the Vatican, or the Library of Congress being made available all around the world on reels of film the size of a person's hand.

By the end of his life, in 1932, Reginald Fessenden was an inventor with more than five hundred patents. However, many of his ideas were too far ahead of their time to be appreciated. For example, in 1919 he patented a device that could transmit voice and pictures. At the time no one was interested, but the Englishman John Baird later became famous for the same kind of invention – the television.

Marconi and Fessenden: Rivals to the End

Unlike Guglielmo Marconi, who came from a wealthy family and could easily buy all the equipment he needed, Fessenden often found himself struggling to make a living. As a result, he was disappointed when the Canadian government chose to fund the Italian inventor's telegraph station in Glace Bay, Nova Scotia. The government policy that gave Marconi his monopoly also held back the development of radio in Canada for more than twenty years. After the First World War, Marconi began experiments on sending human voice by radio, twelve long years after Fessenden's famous Christmas Eve broadcast.

Chapter 7

Just Tune In: Rogers's Batteryless Radio

In the early 1920s, radio quickly went from a fad to a household mainstay. Everyone wanted to own a radio, and people often spent several months' salary on this new luxury item. The early models were boxy contraptions with one or more sets of headphones for listening and sometimes a loudspeaker shaped like a horn. They operated with the power of large batteries, which were sometimes placed on the floor under a table. After a few hours of use, these batteries, which were heavy and expensive to replace, would start to run down, and the radio would begin to make loud screeching sounds.

So why didn't people just plug in their radios? Even though homes had electric power in the early 1920s, the radio was not plugged into an electrical outlet until Edward Samuel Rogers invented a new type of vacuum tube. Before him, no one had been able to make a radio work properly using electric current because it produced so much interference noise that listening to a broadcast would have been impossible.

Until Rogers invented his vacuum tube, people conserved their battery power by waiting until their favorite programs came on before they turned on the radio – otherwise they would risk missing the end of a baseball game or a comedy hour! Even so, reception in the early days was often so poor that newspaper cartoons at the time poked fun at the radio craze by depicting listeners who laughed at jokes they hadn't even heard over the hiss and crackle of interference.

Growing Up with Radio

Like many boys of his generation, Ted Rogers grew up reading articles about how to build your own radio receiver, and

Did you know that in 1923, sales of radios skyrocketed? By the end of that year, more than 400,000 North American families owned a radio. The year before, only 60,000 had.

he often spent time tinkering with crystal sets, an early type of radio. By the time he was eleven, he had already surrounded himself with amateur radio equipment in his parents' elegant Toronto home. Then, in 1914, he was fiddling with his homemade wireless set when he tuned in to a distant radio station and heard the news that England had declared war on Germany. This report had not yet made it into the papers, and the fourteen-year-old made the news for announcing the start of the First World War.

When he was twenty-one, Rogers entered an American Radio Relay League competition for amateur radio operators who wanted to try sending a signal across the Atlantic Ocean to Scotland. A number of young men from points along the East Coast of the United States succeeded in contacting Scotland, but their signals mostly crossed water (which was easier than transmitting across large areas of land). Rogers had a talent for technical precision, and he demonstrated it when his radio signal reached the inland town of Ardrossan, Scotland, from

Crystal Sets and Electron Tubes

When you turn on your radio, it receives the messages via electromagnetic waves that pass through the air. Radio signals must be sent through the atmosphere by a transmitter, usually a radio station, and then captured by a receiver, which makes them audible to the human ear.

The crystal set was an early kind of radio receiver. It detected signals with a small piece of lead crystal, called galena, connected to a thin wire called a cat's whiskers. When electricity traveled through the wire to the crystal, a message could be heard faintly with headphones. Finicky crystal sets were soon replaced by more sensitive receivers that used electron tubes. Also called vacuum tubes, these devices looked like light bulbs – right down to the filament inside. They allowed radio signals to be strengthened and amplified, making them easier to hear clearly.

Today it is hard to imagine the nuisance of replacing the fussy electronic tubes that used to be part of every radio set. However, during radio's early days people came to value tubes that were reliable, because clarity of sound depended on quality tubes. Also, the first electronic tubes depended on battery current to heat the filament and pick up the signal, so a radio tube was only as good as its power source. Unfortunately, batteries ran down all too quickly and were costly to replace. As consumers began to tire of the constant expense of maintaining their radios, sales began to drop off.

Did you know that the Rogers family were Quakers? Ted Rogers's ancestor Thomas came to America on the Mayflower, and soon the family had spread across Pennsylvania and Massachusetts. During the American Revolution, part of the family moved north to a Quaker settlement in Newmarket, Ontario.

Newmarket, Ontario. His signal had traveled farther than anyone else's – and in more difficult conditions.

When Rogers became interested in finding a way to run radios from electricity (that is, with an alternating current, or AC), instead of batteries (a direct current, or DC), engineers argued that it would be impossible to prevent the annoying noise that would result. Rogers had heard that someone named F. S. McCullogh had been trying to solve the problem in Pittsburgh, and he decided to visit him to see the new kind of tube he was working on. McCullogh had indeed invented a new vacuum tube, but it did exactly what the engineers had predicted: generated noisy interference that made it impossible to hear a program properly. Although his friends advised him not to, Rogers bought the rights to McCullogh's patent and began to test methods for solving the problems with its design. His early efforts were discouraging, and everything he tried failed.

Rogers's first success came with the invention of a tube called a **rectifier**. A rectifier turns alternating current into direct current. This rectifier was used to eliminate one of the batteries that radio sets required, the B battery. This was a step in the right direction, but Rogers's goal was to be able to operate a radio with no batteries at all, and this was a more difficult problem to solve.

After a frustrating sequence of trials and failures, Rogers found a method that showed some hope of success. He brought the electrical wires, or leads, out of the top end of the radio tube, keeping them separate from the wires that were already located at the socket end at the bottom of the tube. There was still another problem. When electricity was brought through the tube, it did what it was meant to do: heat the filament. But it was too hot. When he devised an insulator that protected the filament from this excessive heat, he finally had a new AC radio tube that could be manufactured in large quantities and sold to the public for a reasonable price. In the spring of 1925, he applied for a patent for the batteryless radio.

The Batteryless Era

Ted Rogers was not only an inventor with a great idea, he was also a shrewd businessman who had the sense to turn it into an everyday product that people could buy for their homes. He formed one company to manufacture his AC radio tube and another to make the Majestic radio, which featured his tube and did not require batteries. The first of these radios was put on display at the Canadian National Exhibition in 1925.

The batteryless radio boasted excellent reception and, best of all, no batteries; it was meant to be plugged into the same ordinary light socket that already existed in homes. By now, radios were also much more attractive than the early boxy type. The new models were enclosed in cabinets that were designed to be elegant pieces of furniture for the modern home.

Unfortunately, Rogers quickly found that he was the victim of sabotage. The filaments in his tubes were burning out too fast, and customers were upset by the fact that the AC tube didn't last long before it needed to be replaced. Rogers discovered that the wire filament for his tubes was supplied to him by a company that supported one of his competitors. When he changed to a European supplier, the problem of faulty filaments disappeared. After this experience, he increased the security at his plant.

In 1927, by the time he held the patent for the AC radio tube, Rogers was already hard at work on a new invention. Radio stations at the time usually ran for as long as their battery power lasted and then signed off. Rogers remedied this problem by creating the first batteryless radio broadcasting station.

Did you know that as a young man, Rogers worked on inventions in his own laboratory? His family wanted him to go into business, but he preferred to work at his homemade broadcasting station.

The station, which was called CFRB, still exists today. The R stands for "Rogers" and the B for "batteryless." (Some people think the C and the F stand for "Canada's First.") The practice of using call letters that stood for something lasted only a short time, but several Canadian radio stations took advantage of this opportunity to advertise their company through the name of the station.

CFRB shared a radio channel, or frequency, with CKGW, which was owned by the Gooderham and Worts liquor distillery. In those days, very few channels were available, and co-operation between broadcasters was part of the effort of survival. On one occasion, CFRB was ready to sign off so that CKGW could begin its programming when a call came in saying that the distillery's transmitter wasn't working. CFRB was able to stay on the air to transmit CKGW's program.

Did you know that in the first years of broadcasting, CFRB would have about an hour of programming in the morning, another hour in the afternoon, and a longer program in the evening, often featuring dance music from local ballrooms? Twenty-four-hour programming would be a thing of the future.

Did you know that Rogers went on to work on radar in the late 1930s? Sadly, he died suddenly of an aneurysm, leaving his young wife and a son, Edward Samuel, who later continued his father's work in communications.

Many radio stations were first set up in homes, with curtains hung all around the rooms that were used as studios. Often they were started by companies that sold radios and wanted to give people something to listen to while purchasing a new set. There was no practical way of recording programs ahead of time, so shows were live and things often went wrong. For example, one man who sold radios and had his own station left his children in charge of changing records so that the customers in his store could listen to music. Unfortunately, his children tripped over some cords, and instead of music, the crashing sounds of falling equipment and children were broadcast live in the store!

Did you know that because not every home had electricity, there were AC/DC radios that could run with either batteries or electric current?

Sound Effects Men

Radio dramas required convincing sound effects, and soon radio stations were full of a whole assortment of junk used for creating just the right smash, crash, creak, or rumble. Some things were built specially, like door frames that could vary the pitch and echo of a slammed door. Coconut shells were "walked" across gravel to sound like horses, steel sheets were wobbled to make thunder, and cornstarch boxes were squeezed to sound like someone walking through snow. As microphones and amplifiers improved, different techniques were needed to create a realistic sound effect. Eventually, whole libraries of sounds were recorded and sold to radio stations around the world.

Chapter 8

Sending Pictures Through the Air by Wirephoto

In the 1920s, William Samuel Stephenson combined his fascination with new technology with his love of radio to invent the wirephoto, an accurate way of transmitting pictures around the world in seconds. His invention was so successful that he became a millionaire before he was thirty years old. Yet Stephenson is rarely remembered as a scientist and inventor. Instead, most people think of him as the man called Intrepid, one of the greatest spies of the twentieth century.

Because William Stephenson became an important spy, a legend, or false biography, was created about his early life in Canada. A spy's legend mixes fact and fiction to create a story that is just inaccurate enough to mislead an enemy. For instance, Stephenson's "official" biography gives the wrong names and occupations for his parents, his own wrong birthdate and birth name, and even misidentifies the schools he attended. In fact, most of the information about his early life and teenage years was distorted.

What seems to be true is that Stephenson was born William Samuel Clouston Stanger in Winnipeg, Manitoba, on January 23, 1897. His father died when William was only three or four years old, and his mother was not able to support herself and three children, so when William, who was the oldest child, was four, he went to live with the Stephensons, family friends. They adopted him, and his name became William Samuel Stephenson.

The young Stephenson was interested in math, science, and technology. He was studious and had a photographic memory, and he loved to read. In his spare time, he experimented with electricity, kites, steam, and telegraphy. He built his own telegraph, communicating with ships on the Great Lakes, and spent a lot of time on his **ham radio**.

Did you know that on the night of April 14, 1912, Stephenson received the SOS message from the Titanic as it was sinking in the Atlantic Ocean? He told people about it, but they were too far away to help the ship.

Did you know that when he was a child, Stephenson helped capture an escaped murderer? While delivering telegrams in Winnipeg, he saw the wanted man and notified police. They recaptured the fugitive and arrested five more men for helping him escape.

When he was only twelve, Stephenson began working for the Great North West Telegraph Company in Winnipeg.

In the summer of 1914, the First World War began. Stephenson wanted to join the armed forces and fight, but he was too young. Finally, on January 12, 1916, he enlisted. In his enlistment papers, he gave his birthdate as January 11, 1896, because soldiers had to be twenty to be sent overseas.

While he was fighting in the trenches in Europe, Stephenson was injured in a gas attack and sent to England to recuperate. There, he studied navigation, communications, internal combustion engines, and the theory of flight. He also met and talked with other Allied soldiers and officers, often discussing the German military and its movements. Stephenson was very good at analyzing these movements and correctly figuring out German strategy.

While he was recovering, Stephenson also learned to fly airplanes. Even though he had been labeled "disabled for life," he persuaded the Royal Air Force to let him join. When he first arrived, the orderly officer thought he still looked too ill to be any good. But Stephenson became a respected "air ace," shooting down an estimated twenty-six enemy aircraft, including one piloted by Lothar von Richthofen, the brother of the famed Red Baron.

During one of his missions, Stephenson flew to the aid of an Allied pilot who was under attack by seven enemy biplanes. He shot down three of the attackers and the other four retreated, but when he approached the Allied plane to identify himself, the confused pilot fired on him. Stephenson was shot in the leg and crashed his plane behind enemy lines. The Germans captured him and put him in a prison camp.

Stephenson tried to escape several times, but he always got caught. Then he decided to exaggerate his injuries. He gained the trust of his captors by convincing them that he was too disabled to escape. They gave him a job in the kitchen, and this allowed him access to utensils he could use to help him escape. After three months, he was successful. He made his way to the Allies and was rescued. Stephenson received many awards for his bravery and accomplishments during the war, including the Distinguished Flying Cross, the Military Cross, and the French Legion of Honor and Croix de Guerre avec Palme (War cross with palm).

Spy Gadgets

Like many of us, Stephenson liked gadgets and interesting mechanical things. Ian Fleming, the author of the James Bond novels, was a friend and colleague of Stephenson's. He used some of his friend's real-life missions as the basis for Bond's adventures, and he consulted Stephenson about the gadgets that Bond uses in the books. Some of Stephenson's real spy gadgets were tiny cameras, pens that squirted dangerous chemicals, and plastic animal dung that exploded. Always a perfectionist, Stephenson even consulted with professors at the London Zoo to make sure the dung looked real.

The Conquering Hero Returns

When the First World War ended, Stephenson returned home to Winnipeg. He was modest, and didn't tell even his family and friends about his heroics and the medals he'd received. Instead, he turned his attention to business and communications. His childhood interest in telegraphy had matured into a fascination with the relatively new invention of radio. This technology gave him an idea. If sounds could be transmitted clearly through wires (with the telephone) and across the air (via radio), he thought, then surely pictures could too.

The idea of sending pictures over distance was not new. In fact, scientists had been working on transmitting images over telegraph wires since the middle of the nineteenth century. Some had succeeded, but the process was slow, costly, and worked better with line drawings and handwriting than with photographs. Sometimes, telegraph messages appeared in the lines of the photograph.

Stephenson wanted to be able to send any picture or photograph quickly, clearly, and inexpensively. Since he was trained in radio technology and telegraphy, he analyzed the methods that had been used and came up with a new way to scan and transmit photographs.

Stephenson's device used discs and light. The discs were Nipkow discs, which had been invented by a German physicist, Paul Gottlieb Nipkow, in the 1880s. These discs had slits cut in at precise points. Stephenson arranged two Nipkow discs so they overlapped each other, and he synchronized their rotation. The pairs of slits continuously lined up, and when a bright light shone on the disks, a beam moved through the slits and across the photograph to be scanned. The discs rotated so quickly that the light would touch every spot on the picture. Once it had moved across one way, the light dropped down and moved back in the opposite direction until it had scanned the whole image. As it passed over each spot, it was converted into an electrical current.

The paler the area, the more light it reflected back (so very light areas created a greater electrical charge than dark areas). At the other end, a receiver "read" the electrical signals and converted them back into the exact shades of light and dark that were in the original picture. The whole process took twenty seconds, produced a clear and accurate image, and was far less expensive than any previous attempts. And the signals could be transmitted by either radio or telephone.

Stephenson tried to get financial backing for his experiments. Unfortunately, there was no support for his idea at home in Canada, but the British were interested. The *London Daily Mail* had been experimenting with wireless photographic transmission since the early 1900s, but with no success. Lord Northcliffe, the owner of the newspaper, was impressed with Stephenson's ideas, and he provided financial backing and a place for him to experiment. By April 1923, Stephenson had made working models of his device, demonstrated it, and proved it to be faster than any other apparatus then available. He received a patent on July 17, 1924.

A New Era Begins

On December 22, 1924, the *London Daily Mail* published a portrait of King George V that had been transmitted by wirephoto. The newspaper hailed it as "a great scientific event" and claimed that "a new era in illustrated journalism [was] beginning." Stephenson originally called his invention a light-sensitive device, perhaps because the name wirephoto was already used to refer to the earlier inventions. But the word "wirephoto" caught on, and soon Stephenson's invention was so popular that he became a millionaire. Because it was the first affordable, accurate, workable method of transmitting photographs, it revolutionized journalism.

Stephenson was an astute businessman, and he used much of the money he earned from the wirephoto to invest in companies around the world. Eventually, he owned automobile manufacturing plants, oil refineries, coal mines, steel factories, and the largest film studio in the world outside Hollywood. He also owned companies that made engines, aircraft, cement, radios, plastics, and buildings. But since he was always most interested in science and technology, especially communications technology, he still conducted experiments. He worked on laser beams, experimented with putting sound on films (movies were silent until 1927), and helped develop the Spitfire airplane (which was used in the Second World War).

Stephenson was now a wealthy international businessman, and he met politicians, actors, bankers, industrialists, military personnel, and other business people on his travels. It is at this point that the most interesting part of his life begins.

In the 1930s, the Nazis came to power in Germany. Several of Stephenson's friends from the First World War were now in powerful

V for Victory

Stephenson loved music. One day, he realized that if the opening bars of Beethoven's Fifth Symphony were translated into Morse code, they made the letter V. He connected the letter with "victory" over the Nazis, and told Winston Churchill about it. Churchill liked this so much that every British radio broadcast was required to open with the first bars of Beethoven's Fifth as a secret signal to boost morale.

positions in England, and they suspected that Germany was secretly preparing for war. Stephenson agreed. Since his position as a respected international businessman took him to many places around the world, he was able to engage, undetected, in information-gathering activities. As he traveled, Stephenson paid attention to the politics and events taking place in different countries, and he reported his observations through secret channels to Winston Churchill in England.

Stephenson's work was dangerous, however, and it was important that he be as anonymous as possible in his spying. So after 1935, all the records of his activities were erased. Stephenson had to stop contacting his family and friends in Canada without even explaining why – they learned about his espionage work only when books and articles about him appeared after the war. Newspaper clippings were burned, government files were destroyed, and business records were no longer kept about him. There could be no personal information left for the Nazis to use against him.

Stephenson began having secret meetings with Churchill, and he became involved in plans to try to slow down the Nazis. But by 1938, he suspected that war was imminent. Then, on September 1, 1939, Germany invaded Poland and the Second World War began. Although the United States was still neutral, Churchill decided that Britain needed a secret intelligence service (or spy network) on the other side of the Atlantic to help him communicate with President Franklin Roosevelt. He asked William Stephenson to set up and lead this organization, which was to be called the British Security Co-ordination (BSC). Stephenson's code name was Intrepid.

The Quiet Canadian

Stephenson needed a "cover" occupation to explain his presence in the U.S., so he was named the director of the British Passport Office. He established the BSC's secret headquarters in Rockefeller Center, in New York City. Thousands of people worldwide worked with the organization, including well-known writers and actors such as Roald Dahl, Noel Coward, Cary Grant, and Greta Garbo.

In addition to its numerous secretaries, clerks, and spies, Stephenson's organization had multilingual translators and financial experts who could interpret the way organizations

Codes and Ciphers

Throughout history, codes have been used to communicate secret information. Industries use them to guard business secrets and armies send coded orders to keep the enemy from knowing their movements.

The science of inventing codes is called cryptography, from the Greek words cryptos (for "hidden") and graphos (meaning "writing"). Every code needs a key to unlock it. The science of decoding messages without the key is called cryptanalysis.

Technically, codes and ciphers are different. In a code, words, phrases, or messages are replaced by different words, symbols, or letters. Translating a message into code is called encoding it. A cipher, however, replaces every letter, number, or symbol in a message with a different letter, number, or symbol. Translating the original message is called enciphering it.

You can make an alphabet cipher to send your own secret messages. First, print the twenty-six letters of the alphabet across a page. Underneath this, print the alphabet again, starting with any letter other than A. Next, print the message you want to send (the "plaintext"). Encipher it by replacing each letter with the corresponding letter in the second row. You can leave spaces between words or put in dashes to separate them. In this example, the alphabet is moved forward by five letters.

A B C D E F G H I J K L M N O P Q R S T U V W X Y Z
F G H I J K L M N O P Q R S T U V W X Y Z A B C D E

Plaintext: LET'S GO TO THE MOVIES ON SATURDAY
Enciphered: QJYX-LT-YT-YMJ-RTANJX-TS-XFYZWIFD

were using money and other resources to support the enemy. Most of the workers at the BSC were Canadian recruits. They were often hired through newspaper advertisements asking for secretarial workers for a department of the British government in New York City. Many secretaries and clerks did not know what their real jobs were going to be until they got to New York. The BSC even gave them a place to live, monitored their social lives, and paid them in cash (so there were no payroll records).

Much of the BSC's activities revolved around cryptography, the science of deciphering and inventing secret codes. BSC workers intercepted enemy messages, decoded them, and passed the information on to the appropriate officials. The Allies were able to steal enemy secrets, send spies into enemy territory to sabotage Nazi missions, and pass misinformation

The Navajo Code Talkers

During the First World War, the Germans routinely intercepted Allied messages and decoded them. The Allies knew they needed to find new ways to send and receive information, but how? One evening, a captain overheard some of his Native soldiers speaking to each other in their Choctaw language. This gave him the idea that the Germans wouldn't be able to decode messages in North American Native languages.

It wasn't until after the war that the German military identified the strange Allied war codes as Native languages. It sent German spies to North America, where they pretended to be tourists and professors interested in Native culture. If there was another war, the Germans knew they'd be able to identify the language and decode the messages. The spies studied many North American tribes – but not the Navajo.

After the Japanese attacked Pearl Harbor on December 7, 1941, the Americans entered the Second World War. They needed a fast, accurate, and unbreakable code to send messages, and they decided to devise one based on Navajo. Twenty-nine Navajo Natives were recruited for this "special duty."

Each Navajo band speaks a slightly different dialect, so the soldiers' first task was deciding which one to use. Eventually, they picked twenty-six Navajo words to stand in for the letters of the English alphabet. The Navajo word wol-la-chee, for example, which means "ant," stood for the letter A. The word shush, which means "bear," stood for B, and so on. Since code breakers look for frequently repeated letters, words, and sequences of words, the Navajo soldiers eventually gave most English letters three possible Navajo substitutes. By the end of the war, there were sixty-two Navajo words representing alphabet letters and 411 words substituting for military, technical, and frequently used terms.

Navajo is an oral language, not a written one, so the soldiers were accustomed to memorizing what they heard. When a Code Talker, as the soldiers came to be called, received a message, he translated it in his head and delivered it in Navajo code over a field telephone or a radio to another Code Talker at headquarters. This Code Talker listened to the message and wrote down the English translation. Code Talkers became so adept that they could code, send, receive, decode, and deliver messages in less than three minutes. At the time, most code machines took four hours to do the same thing.

Eventually, 375 to 420 Navajo soldiers worked as Code Talkers during the Second World War. Because of the success of the code, the military decided to keep any information about it secret. Code Talkers weren't even allowed to tell their families what they had done during the war. Finally, in 1969, information about the Navajo Code Talkers and their great contribution to the war effort became public.

Did you know that the BSC received communications from all over the world? During the Battle of Midway in the Pacific Ocean, coded messages to Japanese battleships were intercepted. The Allies discovered their positions, moved their warplanes quickly, bombed the ships, and won the battle.

back to the Nazis to mislead them into changing their plans. The BSC set up security patrols at railroads, shipping docks, and harbors, and monitored mail between the United States and Europe. Workers found ways to open sealed envelopes, read and decode letters, and reseal them so that the recipient couldn't tell the letter had been tampered with. In this way, the BSC was able to uncover many spies and Nazi sympathizers in the U.S.

During the war, Stephenson also co-ordinated dangerous missions and directed spies – and he even went on missions himself. His own invention, the wirephoto, was used to quickly and accurately transmit photographs of enemy stations and movements.

Stephenson also helped set up a school for secret agents on the north shore of Lake Ontario, near Oshawa. Its official name was Special Training School 103 (STS 103), but it was known as Camp X. At Camp X, agents learned how to steal secrets, blend in to the background when following people, use explosives, make fake passports, read maps, and send and receive coded messages. The school also had a large communications center, which was the brainchild of Benjamin de Forest Bayly, a brilliant engineering professor from Toronto. A huge underground radio transmitter sent and received top-secret messages twenty-four hours a day. By 1943, it was the largest radio-communications unit in the world. Bayly called it Hydra, after the mythical Greek monster with many heads.

During the war, Stephenson never received a salary. In fact, he spent more than a million dollars of his own money for the BSC. After the war, King George VI knighted him in honor of his great service, and President Harry Truman presented him with the Presidential Medal of Merit. Sir William received countless other awards and honors, and a number of books were written about his work in espionage. He became known as the Quiet Canadian for both his work and his modesty.

When the war ended, Stephenson returned to his businesses and worked at helping poor countries develop industries. Officials from Western governments and organizations continued to consult with him about intelligence information, however. Until his death in Bermuda in 1989, he continued to follow world events, send and receive daily messages, and visit with friends and officials. Although he was famous for his wartime activities, Stephenson wished more than anything that all people would join together to fight "poverty, disease, and ignorance," instead of each other.

Chapter 9

Sending Messages Through Space by Satellite

On the evening of November 9, 1972, the rocket containing the communications satellite *Anik A-1* stood on the launchpad at Cape Canaveral, Florida, preparing to blast into space. The countdown began. Then, at six minutes to launch, everything stopped. People were boating on the water! Officials set out to shoo them away so the area would be clear for *Anik*'s takeoff. They worked fast. If *Anik A-1* didn't launch between 7:30 p.m. and 8:33 p.m., it wouldn't achieve its proper position in orbit. As soon as the area was clear, the countdown continued and *Anik* blasted off. Two months later, twenty-five remote communities in northern Canada saw television for the first time.

Ready for Takeoff

Canada's interest in space preceded the *Anik* launch by ten years and was prompted by disrupted communications signals on earth. Scientists determined that disturbances in a layer of the atmosphere called the **ionosphere** interfered with telephone and television signals. The ionosphere is made up of electrically charged particles called ions and electrons. Without this layer, low-energy signals would go straight out into space instead of being reflected back to earth. But sometimes the sun

Did you know that one of the most obvious disturbances in the ionosphere is the aurora borealis, or northern lights? The northern lights are actually the result of a solar storm in space, and they used to knock out all communications in the Far North. In fact, as recently as 1989 a magnetic storm in the ionosphere caused a power blackout throughout the province of Quebec.

would disrupt the ionosphere, and radio signals would escape into space anyway. These solar disturbances were frequent and unpredictable.

Since changes in the ionosphere affected communications in the North, Canadian scientists decided to build a satellite to probe the ionosphere and learn more about it. Even though what was then the Soviet Union and the U.S. already each had a satellite in space, this was still a new science. No one had much experience building space vehicles, and scientists in other countries thought Canada would be unsuccessful. But on September 29, 1962, a rocket carrying the first Canadian satellite, *Alouette,* blasted off. On that day, Canada became the third country in space.

When *Alouette* began transmitting data to earth, however, there was a shock. Scientists at the U.S. National Aeronautics and Space Agency (NASA) were unprepared. They confessed that they had secretly believed *Alouette* would fall apart shortly after getting into space, so they hadn't established a system to receive and measure the information it transmitted. It took some fancy footwork to get something up and running quickly. And Canadians discovered just how little confidence other scientists had had in the project.

Alouette worked so well because its designers overprepared their satellite. One of the challenges in satellite design is finding a way to keep the weight low while loading up with the maximum amount of fuel. *Alouette*'s designers decided to use solar power, with batteries for backup. And they requested a powerful rocket to launch it and a booster to put it into orbit once it was in space. Unfortunately, *Alouette*'s designers worked so hard to keep it light that it was too light! Concrete had to be put in the rocket with *Alouette* to make it heavy enough to launch.

Alouette measured cosmic noise, or sounds in space, and used a sonar system to map the top of the ionosphere. It sent out a radar pulse, then received the echo, or reflected pulse. *Alouette* sent more than a million images of the ionosphere to earth, providing scientists with

Did you know that the first satellite transmission was a greeting from President Dwight D. Eisenhower to Prime Minister John Diefenbaker? It happened in 1959, when Diefenbaker was opening the Prince Albert Radar Laboratory, and the greeting was transmitted using the moon, earth's natural satellite. Signals bounced off the moon and were received two and a half seconds later back on earth.

important information about how the sun affects the ionosphere and disrupts earth's radio transmissions. Though *Alouette* was built to last seven years, it lasted ten.

A New Era in Space

Alouette's success impressed scientists all over the globe. Because of it, the United States proposed that Canada and NASA team up to send more scientific research satellites into space. In 1963, the two countries created International Satellites for Ionospheric Studies (ISIS). Canada designed, developed, and built the satellites, and NASA launched them. Soon, other countries joined ISIS. From 1965–71, it sent three satellites into orbit: *Alouette-II, ISIS-I,* and *ISIS-II.* The ISIS satellites lasted twenty years, and *ISIS-II* transmitted the first pictures of the northern lights from above. These satellites collected data from a complete eleven-year solar cycle, giving scientists a much better understanding of ionospheric effects on communication.

Did you know that the International Telecommunications Satellite Organization (INTELSAT) links more than one hundred countries by communications satellites?

In a 1967 report called "Upper Atmosphere and Space Programs in Canada," John Chapman proposed changing the focus of Canada's space program from scientific research to communications. For years, Chapman had been in charge of the teams working on

The Canadarm

When satellites wear out or need repairs, a robotic arm picks them up in space and takes them to the space shuttle's cargo bay. The official name for this robot is the Remote Manipulator System (RMS), but it's usually called the Canadarm. It's designed to act like an arm, with joints that bend and rotate at the shoulder, elbow, and wrist. A cylinder at the end of the arm has three snare wires to grasp a grapple fixture at the end of satellites, much as a hand grabs a handle. Astronauts operate the Canadarm by remote control from inside the space shuttle. The first Canadarm rocketed into space on the space shuttle Columbia on November 13, 1981. It worked so well that NASA invited Canada to send astronauts on later shuttle missions.

A more advanced version of the Canadarm is being used today to build the International Space Station (ISS). Canada, the U.S., Russia, the European Space Agency (which has eleven member countries), Japan, and Brazil are all collaborating on the ISS. Once it's finished, it will be an international city where scientists will perform experiments to learn about space and solve problems on earth.

satellite design. He believed that Canadian scientists were in an ideal position to use the information they had gathered about space to improve communications technology on earth. Even the most remote places would be able to receive radio, telephone, and television signals.

The idea of a communications satellite wasn't new. The U.S. had launched *Telstar* in 1962, and the Russians had six satellites orbiting earth by the late 1960s. These satellites moved through space at varying speeds and in different directions, however, so they had to be tracked by antennas and stations on earth that moved to follow them. Chapman proposed something different. Canada would put a satellite into space in a **geosynchronous**

Did you know that the earth turns at 6,900 miles (11,100 km) per hour?

orbit. This meant that the satellite would orbit 22,300 miles (35,900 km) above the earth, taking the same twenty-four-hour period to orbit the earth as earth does to orbit the sun. From earth, the satellite would appear to be in the same position in space all the time. In reality, it would speed up or slow down to match the earth's orbit.

Geosynchronous satellites, also called geostationary satellites, generally move in an elliptical, or egg-shaped, orbit. As the satellite moves, many forces act on it, including gravity from the sun, the moon, and the earth. At the top of the ellipse, or egg shape, the satellite is closest to earth and must move faster to combat its gravity and not get pulled closer to the planet. This is called the perigee of its orbit. The spot farthest from earth is called the satellite's apogee.

Types of Satellites

There are nine basic types of satellites providing us with information from space:

- astronomy satellites send data about planets and stars;
- atmospheric studies satellites send information about the earth's atmosphere;
- communications satellites transmit signals from one place on earth to another;
- navigation satellites help ships calculate their location on the sea;
- reconnaissance satellites spy on other countries for the military;
- remote-sensing satellites provide data about the environment;
- search-and-rescue satellites receive beams from emergency devices and direct rescuers to accidents;
- space exploration satellites probe the solar system; and
- weather satellites allow meteorologists to know what the weather is at any spot on earth at any time.

Putting Our "Little Brother" in Orbit

Communications satellites use microwaves to send and receive information. Essentially, they take the place of our earth-bound microwave relay towers, which can be unreliable and cannot transmit signals across oceans. Put simply, a satellite is like a huge microwave tower. It can be used in places where it is either too expensive or too difficult to install land-based communications.

Microwave beams don't spread much as they travel, the way sound waves do, and because they have a very high frequency, they can carry a lot of information with little power. (In fact, solar cells supply enough power, with batteries used for backup when the moon or the earth gets between the satellite and the sun, blocking the sun's rays.) A microwave signal from earth is beamed at a satellite's receiving antenna. The satellite receives the signal (which has

See How Communications Satellites Work

More than 120 geosynchronous communications satellites currently circle the earth's equator, traveling so quickly that they complete an orbit in twenty-four hours. They work by reflecting signals from a transmitter on earth to a receiver at a different place. Satellites can reflect signals to anywhere on the planet, and this simple experiment shows how.

You will need:

- a flashlight
- a flat mirror (or one with a stand)
- modeling clay (if your mirror has no stand)
- a portable table
- a piece of black construction paper
- a helper

To Make Your Satellite

Place the table near an open door. Use the modeling clay to hold the mirror in an upright position on the table (or use a mirror with its own stand).

Have your helper go through the open door and find a position where he or she can see the mirror but cannot see you.

Shine the flashlight at the mirror (the satellite). Move around until you find a position where your helper (the receiver) can see the light but cannot see you (the transmitter). Change the position of the mirror and find new positions that work.

You and your helper can also do an experiment in the same room. One of you holds the flashlight while the other one holds the piece of black construction paper in a vertical position. Both of you should stand where you can see the mirror and each other.

Shine the light on the mirror. Both of you move until the light from the flashlight reflects off the mirror onto the black paper. You may need to get very close to the mirror to do this.

The way the light moves from the flashlight to the mirror, then reflects off the mirror to your helper's eyes and the construction paper is similar to the way satellites send communications transmissions around the earth.

weakened over distance), boosts it, and sends it back to earth, where it is amplified again and sent on. Signals sent back from a satellite can be received by many different locations at the same time. And since microwaves travel at the speed of light, this all happens very quickly – there's only about a quarter-second delay between transmission and reception.

After Chapman released his report, the Canadian government decided to establish Telesat Canada to design and build the country's satellites. Right away, Telesat scientists got busy designing their first communications satellite, and the company invited people from all across Canada to name it. The winning entry was Anik, which means "little brother" in Inuit. The name suggested the important role telecommunications would play in bringing Canadians together.

With the successful launch of *Anik A-1,* Canada became the first country with a domestic communications satellite system in geosynchronous orbit. Sixty-three days after its launch, it was in use. And on January 11, 1973, the remote Arctic villages of Frobisher Bay and Resolute telephoned southern Canada by using the *Anik* satellite. By that spring, twenty-five communities in the North were receiving television for the first time. *Anik*'s footprint (that is, the area it could reach) was all of Canada. It saw the whole country from space and could connect any number of spots, no matter how far apart. *Anik* had twelve channels, or transponders. Each transponder was capable of carrying 960 telephone calls or one television channel.

Originally, Canada was assigned three spots in orbit. (Every geosynchronous satellite is assigned a specific spot above the equator – it's like a parking place in space.) As each satellite wore out, it was removed from its spot and a new one put in its place. In the year 2000, *Anik F-1* was launched. It can carry 132 television signals, or thousands of telephone calls or radio signals. *Anik F-1* will service all of North and South America.

All of the Anik satellites lasted longer than expected, even though *Anik E-1* had its southern solar panel ripped off in an electromagnetic storm in space. Before the Anik satellites, bad weather and changes in the earth's atmosphere would cut off communications to the North for weeks at a time. The Aniks not only reduced the isolation of remote communities, but also brought "real time" television. For the first time, northern communities watched and heard about events as they happened, instead of weeks or even months later.

A Bridge Across Space and Time

During the late 1990s, Telesat began working on a direct-broadcast satellite with a footprint of all of North America. Again there was a national contest for a name, and this time the winner was Nimiq. This is an Inuit word that describes an object or force that unites things or binds them together. On May 20, 1999, Telesat launched *Nimiq.*

The success of Telesat's Anik satellites

sparked a joint Canada-U.S. project to experiment with different types of communications by satellite. The two countries wanted to use satellites to bridge distance instantly. Once again, Canada designed and built the satellite, and NASA launched it. This one was named *Hermes,* after the messenger of the gods in Greek mythology. It was ten times more powerful than any previous satellite.

Once *Hermes* was in orbit, Canada and the U.S. both performed experiments using the satellite. Some of the experiments were in tele-education, tele-medicine, and direct-to-home broadcasting. The tele-education experiments involved audio (sound) or video (picture) contact, both one-way and interactively (two-way). The tele-medicine experiments used audio and video links between doctors and patients in remote locations and specialists in major city hospitals. The satellite transmitted data to the city so specialists could offer suggestions, diagnose X-rays, prescribe treatment, and even guide operations. And in 1979, TVOntario used *Hermes* to broadcast educational programs to four schools in remote locations. This was the first direct broadcast by satellite to individual buildings with smaller antennas.

When the experiments with *Hermes* began, one man in Whitehorse, Yukon, was paying close attention. His name was Rolf Hougen, and he owned WHTV, the only television channel in Whitehorse. He wanted to improve television for local residents.

Since it was impossible for the remote community to receive any television signals, film had to be shipped up from southern Canada. It was too expensive to ship film quickly, however, so WHTV viewers routinely got their news and entertainment weeks or months late – like Christmas parades in June. Sometimes, to fill airtime, the station's only television camera just pointed out the window and showed people going in and out of a store across the street.

When Hougen heard about the experiments with the Anik and Hermes communications satellites, he had an idea. Why not use the Anik satellites to broadcast TV to small, isolated communities? Small cable-TV companies could be established in these places, and they could receive the satellite beams and distribute programming to their subscribers. People in remote areas would finally be able to watch TV in real time, just like other Canadians.

Hougen called his proposal "Down to Earth," and he traveled across Canada, at his own expense, trying to get broadcasters and companies to support it. He had expected to find that only inhabitants of isolated communities wanted better TV reception, but he discovered instead that people all across Canada did.

Some pirate earth stations already existed; they received U.S. TV signals and sent them out to subscribers illegally. Hougen knew he needed to act quickly before this trend got bigger, so he and his supporters formed Canadian Satellite Communications Inc. (Cancom). Cancom's goal was to make a satellite-television package available to small communities, thereby bringing more Canadians in contact with each other.

The Canadian government knew about the illegal satellite dishes that were popping up, and it decided that Hougen's idea was good. It invited possible satellite providers to apply for a license to service remote and underserved communities. Cancom applied, as did many other companies. But Hougen had been working on this idea for years, so he announced that Cancom could have its system in place within ninety days. His competitors laughed out loud, but Cancom got the license and went to work.

On July 15, 1981, people gathered in Edmonton, Vancouver, and Whitehorse, waiting for the first commercial satellite broadcast of four television stations. At 3 p.m., Edmonton called, "We see all four signals." Then Vancouver said, "All four signals strong here." And finally, at WHTV, where it all began, a crowd of reporters, government officials, bankers, and businessmen cheered as all four stations went live.

A Dream Fulfilled

Not everyone was happy about satellite television. Some people thought the North didn't really need it; some feared that television would ruin northern culture; and many television stations and movie theaters thought it threatened their businesses. The National Hockey League even tried to stop hockey games from being broadcast by satellite. Like many businesses, Cancom faced these and other challenges head-on, though the company didn't make any profit for almost seven years.

For many people, however, satellite technology acted as just the link between people it was supposed to be. Natives, for example, had had almost no representation in broadcasting before satellite TV. Now they had an opportunity to produce and present programs to communicate their way of life to others.

Eventually, several Native TV stations came together to form Television Northern Canada (TVNC), the world's first aboriginal broadcasting network. Today, TVNC carries programs in seven languages, from more than twelve Native groups across northern Canada. More aboriginal people are involved in broadcasting in Canada than in any other country. Cancom provides free satellite transmission for five Native radio stations and a free satellite uplink for the Whitehorse station, thus making Native TV and radio accessible to many Canadians.

Today, communications satellites play such a large role in our everyday lives that we use them without realizing it. When you watch television, listen to the radio, or make a long-distance telephone call, you are using communications satellite technology. Of course, our communications needs continue to change, and satellite technology promises to become increasingly important in providing high-speed communications over distance – the global link that so many early scientists envisioned.

Chapter 10

Communication at the Speed of Light

Since the invention of the telephone, when Alexander Graham Bell first stretched a simple galvanized wire along the fence posts on his parents' farm, metal cables have carried voice messages down phone lines. Today, information also travels along thin strands of glass, called optical fibers. Unlike metal wire, glass fibers do not conduct electricity, so messages are carried on light waves made by a laser beam.

Early Discoveries

Fiber-optic technology seems so thoroughly modern that it is hard to imagine that its story begins about 150 years ago, with a few simple but important experiments. In 1841, Prof. Daniel Colladon of Geneva, Switzerland, was showing a class of students the dynamics of water flowing out of a hole in a water tank. To make the water jet easier to see, he piped sunlight into the tank, using a lens to focus the beam of light on the hole. What he noticed was that instead of shining straight ahead, the light was trapped in the stream of water and followed it in a curving fountain.

At about the same time, Jacques Babinet of France observed that light could be guided through a glass rod. As an expert on lenses and light, he thought that a rod of bent glass could be used as a guide to shine light into awkward places. However, the kind of glass available at the time was not very pure, and a lot of light was lost before it reached the other end of the rod. Many years would pass before Babinet's discovery began to seem promising.

In London in the 1850s, John Tyndall became well known for light-guiding demonstrations, using a set-up similar to Colladon's. At the time, spectacles featuring fountains

Make Your Own Light Fountain

See for yourself how light will travel through water by trying this easy experiment over the bathroom sink with the lights off. A plastic cup is wrapped in foil so that the light you shine into it is reflected inside the cup. Using a straw to guide the water, you will see small dots bounce on the sink where the light follows the water that spills out of the cup.

You will need:

- a disposable plastic cup
- a straw
- masking tape
- tin foil
- scissors
- a flashlight
- water

To Make the Light Fountain

1. Halfway up the side of the cup, poke a hole with the scissors (have an adult help with this).
2. Push the straw into this hole and cut it so that 1/2 inch (1 cm) is inside the cup and 1 inch (2.5 cm) is sticking out. Use tape to hold the straw in place.
3. Get ready to wrap the cup by cutting a piece of foil (about 8 inches [20 cm] square). Place the cup in the middle of the foil (shiny side up) and measure where the straw will push through. Cut a little hole for the straw and poke it through. Press the rest of the foil up against the cup and over the rim so the whole cup is covered.
4. Have the flashlight turned on and waiting on the counter while you fill the cup with water from the tap. Now shine the light into the top of the cup and watch how it twinkles on the sink where the water spills out.

made up of streams of lighted water were a popular attraction, much like laser shows are today. The experiments of Colladon, Babinet, and Tyndall were just some of the small steps in the march toward the future science of fiber optics.

In 1880, Alexander Graham Bell discovered that voice messages could be carried on a light wave. He called his invention the photophone. It sent sound on a beam of sunlight that was focused on a mirror, and the message was picked up a few feet away by a telephone

Bell's Photophone

On April 1, 1880, Alexander Graham Bell and his associate, Charles Sumner Tainter, first sent a voice message on light. From the roof of a school, Tainter said into the photophone, "Mr. Bell, if you hear what I say, come to the window and wave your hat." In his laboratory 233 yards (213 m) away, Bell heard Tainter and dashed to the window, waving his hat enthusiastically. Bell told people that the photophone was a wireless telephone, and he believed it would be his most important invention.

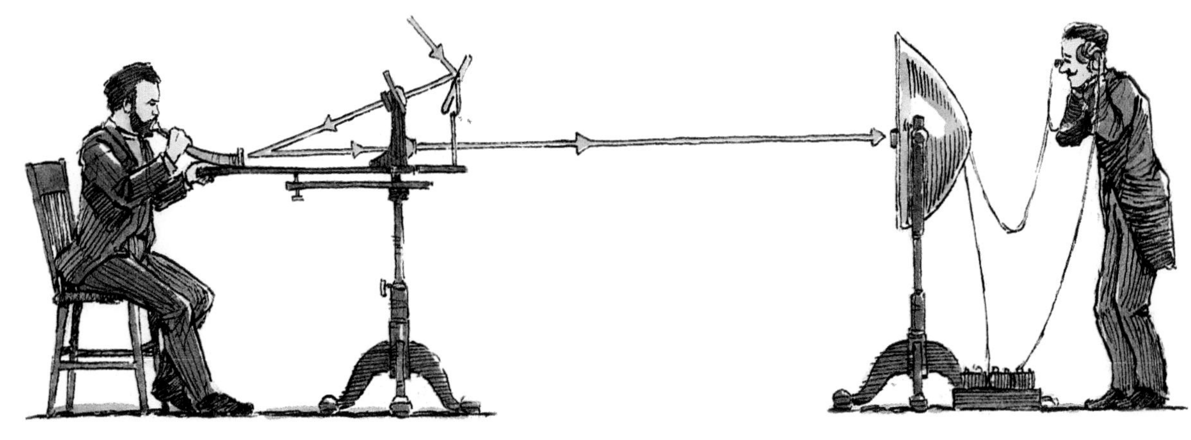

receiver outfitted with a selenium cell. Bell had discovered that the element selenium was sensitive to light, so he used it to measure changes made by sound waves carried on light. This information was then translated into an electric signal that a telephone receiver could turn back into a voice. When he first heard the sound coming through the headphones, Bell said: "I have heard articulate speech produced by sunlight! I have heard a ray of sun laugh and cough and sing."

Bell's invention was not practical for use in the telephone industry in the 1880s because the signal could travel only a short distance. But he had demonstrated that light could be a carrier of voices – just like wires were. He did not recognize that glass could guide light in the photophone, but even if he had, it would have been a poor conductor at the time. It would take decades of research by many scientists before fiber cables would be able to carry

Did you know that scientists have long been interested in using light for communication because light waves have a much higher frequency than even the highest radio frequency? This means that light has more space to carry messages than a lower-frequency carrier like electricity or radio waves.

phone signals across great distances. About a hundred years later, Bell's idea would become reality, but at the time there was no suitable light source, such as a laser, and no way to send a light beam across a distance or around corners without losing too much of the reflected light. Both of these problems have been solved with modern fiber-optic technology.

Solving the Problems

Before light could be used effectively, scientists had to figure out how to send it across a long length of glass fiber and have it arrive without escaping or being absorbed. Improving the quality of the glass used in cables was a top priority, because impurities in ordinary glass absorb light. This isn't a problem with a window because it is so thin, but in a long fiber-optic strand these impurities reduce the amount of light that gets to its destination. The purer the glass fiber, the greater the distance the light will travel. Scientists also had to find a way to prevent the light from escaping to the air when the fiber was bent around corners. This was solved by surrounding the core of the glass fibers with a special covering called a **cladding**. The cladding ensures that light is trapped in the core, and thus that all of the light makes the trip down the path of the cable.

Did you know that the glass used to make fiber-optic cables is one hundred times more pure than the kind used in windows?

Scientists also learned that lasers produce a suitable kind of light for use with an optical fiber. Laser light is used because it can be very focused, unlike ordinary light (which spreads out over a wide area). Laser light has a narrow beam because all of its waves have the same wavelength and travel together in step. Natural light tends to spread out because it is made up of many different wavelengths that don't fit tightly together. With the discovery of lasers and fiber-optic cables, the problems Bell faced with his photophone were solved and communicating with light became a reality.

The Saskatchewan Story

The difficulties of communicating over long distances are most plainly obvious in areas such as the North American prairies, where small towns and cities are spread across a sweeping expanse. So it is not surprising that one leader in fiber-optic systems pioneered this new technology from the mostly rural Canadian province of Saskatchewan. In 1980, SaskTel began installing the first commercial fiber-optics network in the world, and by 1984 this network connected fifty-two cities and towns.

SaskTel partnered with Northern Telecom in 1986 to test new ways to boost the capacity of the phone system. Many homes in Saskatchewan already received cable television through coaxial cable (or coax), which can carry more information traffic than telephone wires. By combining coax with fiber-optic technology, the two companies were able to

Did you know that Saskatchewan has more fiber optics per capita than any other place in the world?

provide video-on-demand service to schools. They called the invention FCH, which stands for fiber-coax hybrid.

FCH used speedy fiber-optic cables to send a signal to a group of homes or an institution, then used cable-television lines (coax) for the last part of the trip (that is, into the individual homes). This was a good way to make use of the existing cable technology, and soon FCH was being used around the world to deliver cable-television and phone services.

SaskTel's invention was first tested as a way to send videos directly into school classrooms without using videotapes or VCRs. A video would be transmitted from the school media center directly to the classroom television, where it was controlled by a new type of Nintendo paddle that allowed viewers to play, pause, rewind, and so on.

Variations of this technology were developed in the 1990s. By then, video could be sent in Hyper Real Time, which meant that a full-length video traveled down a combination of fiber-optic cable and a fast telephone wire (this was called fiber-wire hybrid) in a few minutes instead of an hour and a half. SaskTel also developed a similar system that used high-frequency radio waves for the last part of the journey. Because the signal traveled through the air for the final distance, this was called fiber-air hybrid.

The Ken Hill Story

Working in Ottawa at the Communications Research Centre, Dr. Ken Hill discovered that a beam of laser light sent along a fiber of glass could etch a long wavy path or regular pattern in the glass core. He had been experimenting with a fiber about three feet (1 m) in length, using a lens to aim a laser beam into it. He also used a photo-detector to measure how much light made it to the end of the fiber. Then a strange thing happened. After a short while, less light started coming out of the end. So, Hill asked himself, where was it going? There were only two possibilities: that the light was being absorbed by the fiber, or that it was being reflected back to the other end. A different experiment was needed to test which of these explanations was correct.

To measure how much light was escaping in both directions, Hill set up a photo-detector at each end of the glass fiber. Then, instead of aiming the laser beam straight into the fiber, he bounced it off a semi-transparent mirror. At first, most of the light directed into the fiber went through it and out the other end, but then something changed. The detector at the input end began to show higher amounts of light being reflected back up the fiber. A mirror effect was being created inside the fiber. This mirror turned out to be permanent; it would come undone only if the glass fiber was stretched.

Hill's discovery was that the structure of the

glass in an optical fiber could be changed so that the light would be reflected from a regular pattern created inside the glass. The discovery was called **photosensitivity**, and the pattern markings became known as Bragg gratings (for Sir Lawrence Bragg, who first discovered a similar effect in his experiments with crystals).

In our information society, we want communications systems to carry a lot of data in all formats very quickly. We want, for example, to be able to download video and music files from the Internet. To support such demanding kinds of communication, however, the technology had to change. Copper cables and coax just did not have enough capacity.

Fiber optics added much more capacity to the system, but the invention of photosensitivity meant even fiber could carry more information. And most important, photosensitivity made wavelength division multiplexing (WDM) possible. What does this mean? In an ordinary fiber strand, the light being sent has only one wavelength. However, Bragg gratings allow a single fiber to carry several different beams of light from a number of lasers, combining all the various wavelengths in the journey down the fiber (this is multiplexing). At the destination, the wavelengths are divided up again, and the messages carried by each are detected separately (this is wavelength division). This means that with WDM, more information traffic can be sent along each single optical fiber.

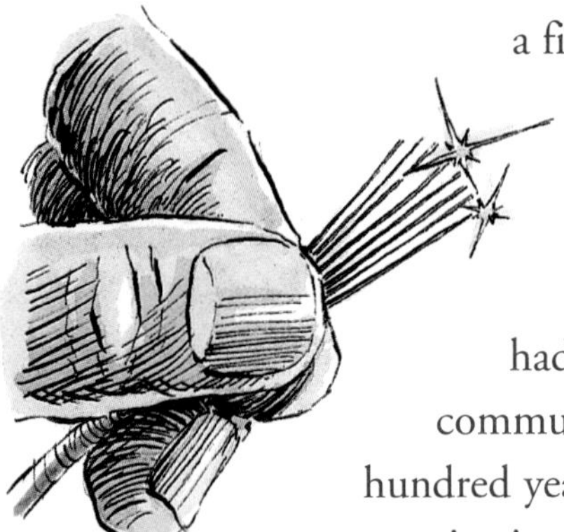

Photosensitivity has also been used to design sensors that can measure strain in physical structures like bridges or aircraft. A fiber-optic cable containing Bragg gratings will be embedded in a bridge to test how well the reinforcing structures stand up to stress over time. When the bridge is affected by changes in heat, for example, the glass fiber will stretch, making the wave pattern of the gratings lengthen slightly (which in turn changes the wavelength of the light that is reflected by the gratings). These changes in the gratings can be measured by a tunable wavelength laser beam sent down the glass cable. Robotics built into the bridge can then adjust to these stresses. This combination of a fiber-optic sensor and robotics is called a smart system.

By the end of the twentieth century, the science of fiber optics had transformed the way we communicate. Over the past two hundred years, the speed of change in communications technology has intensified. It took fifty years to get from Morse's telegraph to Marconi's wireless system, but only twenty-five years separate Bell's telephone and Fessenden's radio success. Today, change is more rapid still – and who knows what the future holds.

Glossary

barretter: a device for detecting radio waves that was able to receive the continuous waves sent by Fessenden's voice radio system.

cladding: a protective covering.

coherer: an instrument for detecting radio waves that had a glass tube filled with iron filings; it was used for Morse code transmissions but did not work for voice radio.

coucher: in papermaking, the person who drains water off the paper mold and removes the damp sheet.

diaphragm: a very thin disk; its vibrations change sounds to electrical current and back again.

electromagnetic waves: a kind of radiation that includes light waves and radio waves and is made up of both electric and magnetic fields.

engraving: carving, cutting, or etching a drawing or letters into a material like stone, metal, wood, or glass.

Fenians: a secret organization devoted to winning Irish independence from Britain; they named themselves after a group of legendary Irish warriors from the first and second centuries.

flammable: easily set on fire.

focal plane: the point where light rays create a clear image of an original scene.

focal point: the point where rays of light cross once they've been bent by a lens.

frequency: all waves, including radio and light waves, have a cycle; the frequency of the wave is the number of times per second that cycle occurs.

geosynchronous: moving at the same rate of speed as earth (a satellite in geosynchronous orbit moves with earth's twenty-four-hour rotation, so it appears to stay in one place at all times).

halftone: a picture made up of tiny dots of different sizes and density that produce different tones (i.e., light and dark); it is produced by photographing an original image through a fine screen.

ham radio: amateur radio, usually using short-wave.

heterodyne principle: in radio science, the process of creating one audible frequency (i.e., the radio broadcast you can hear) from two higher frequencies.

high-frequency alternator: a generator that produced alternating current and was used to generate continuous waves for voice radio.

interrupter: a device that was used with a spark transmitter to send radio signals in the form of Morse code.

ionosphere: a layer of the atmosphere above the stratosphere; the ionosphere is able to reflect radio waves for long-distance transmission around the world.

layman: in papermaking, a worker who removes sheets of paper from between layers of felt after the water has been pressed out of them.

Leggotype: the photoengraving process invented by Georges-Édouard Desbarats and William Leggo; they used it to make halftones and print photographs in newspapers and magazines.

lithograph: a print created from a chemically treated flat surface that holds ink only on the areas to be printed.

papyrus: an Egyptian writing material made with flattened reeds laid out in a criss-cross pattern to form a very thin mat.

patent: a government document giving an inventor exclusive rights to make and sell his or her invention.

photosensitivity: the mirror-like effect created in a glass fiber when a laser beam etches a pattern into it.

receiver: a piece of equipment, such as part of a telephone or a radio, that receives electromagnetic signals and changes them back into sound.

rectifier: a device used to change electricity from alternating current (from an electrical outlet) to direct current (the kind produced by batteries).

resonance: a principle whereby sound produced by an object, like a tuning fork, causes materials that vibrate at the same frequency to make the same sound.

shutter: a cover that opens and closes to allow light to pass through a camera's lens and expose the film.

transmitter: a piece of equipment, such as part of a telephone or a radio, that converts sound into electrical impulses and sends them to a receiver.

vatman: in papermaking, the person who dips the mold into a vat (or large container) filled with mash made from water and plant fibers.

vellum: a fine paper-like material that was used in old manuscripts and was made from calf skin.

woodcut: a piece of wood with a design carved into it; the print made from this is also called a woodcut.

Index

Page numbers in italics refer to illustrations.

Acknowledgments

There are many people we would like to thank for their assistance, which included discussing the technical workings of inventions, helping us to find information, and especially reading and commenting on drafts of the chapters. In particular, we want to thank the following: Aynsley MacFarlane, Alexander Graham Bell National Historic Site; Dr. John S. Belrose, Communications Research Centre, Ottawa; Elliott Sivowitch, Electricity Department, Smithsonian Institution; Tim Lawson; Syd Davy, Intrepid Society of Winnipeg; Douglas Hildebrand, Military Communications and Electronics Museum; Graham C. Bradley, SaskTel; Dr. Ken Hill, Communications Research Centre, Ottawa; Ted Rogers, Rogers Telecommunications; Arthur Eric Zimmerman, CFRC Radio, Kingston; Maureen Lucas; Andrew, Benjamin, and Rebecca Peterson; Christopher and Samantha Dean; Matthew, Michael, Adam, and Ashley Egler; Peggy and Holmes Hooke.

Many people have contributed to this book in other ways, and we wish to offer warm thanks to friends and family members whose interest and enthusiasm has meant so much, especially Glen, Tim, and Paul. We would also like to thank Bill Slavin, who interpreted our text so well in his illustrations, our editor, Janice Weaver, and our publisher, Kathy Lowinger. Any errors that escaped attention are our responsibility.